Homofiles

Homofiles

Theory, Sexuality, and Graduate Studies

Edited by Jes Battis

LEXINGTON BOOKS
Lanham • Boulder • New York • Toronto • Plymouth, UK

Published by Lexington Books
A wholly owned subsidiary of The Rowman & Littlefield Publishing Group, Inc.
4501 Forbes Boulevard, Suite 200, Lanham, Maryland 20706
www.lexingtonbooks.com

Estover Road, Plymouth PL6 7PY, United Kingdom

British Library Cataloguing in Publication Information Available

Library of Congress Cataloging-in-Publication Data
Homofiles : theory, sexuality, and graduate studies / [edited by] Jes Battis.
p. cm.
ISBN 978-0-7391-3191-6 (cloth : alk. paper)
1. Queer theory. 2. Sex (Psychology) 3. Gay and lesbian studies. 4. Lesbian college students. 5. Gay college students. 6. Transgender college students. I. Battis, Jes, 1979–
HQ76.25.H643 2010
306.76'6—dc22 2011022271

∞™ The paper used in this publication meets the minimum requirements of American National Standard for Information Sciences—Permanence of Paper for Printed Library Materials, ANSI/NISO Z39.48-1992.

Printed in the United States of America

Contents

Introduction

Homofiles: Desire, Praxis, and Pedagogy

Jes Battis

> "I came to theory because I was hurting—the pain within me was so intense that I could not go on living . . . [I] saw in theory then a location for healing (59)."
>
> —bell hooks, *Teaching to Transgress*

> "Graduate students are my sexual preference."
>
> —Jane Gallop

In the early- to mid-1990s, there was a dramatic boiling over of interest in the work of queer graduate students, as if public desire had been fomenting until now within the academy and finally couldn't be contained any longer. Various high-profile conferences devoted to queer grads were successfully hosted throughout middle-America, the most infamous undoubtedly being the 1991 "Flaunting It" conference at the University of Wisconsin-Milwaukee, also the first conference of its kind. It was there that, when asked about her sexuality—possibly while wearing her legendary skirt made of men's silk ties all sewn together, like the skin of her flayed victims—Jane Gallop was said to have proclaimed that "graduate students are my sexual preference." Two years later, she was caught in a well-publicized sexual harassment suit after kissing one of her female graduate students (she was later cleared of all charges), which spawned a best-selling 1997 book with Duke University Press, *Feminist Accused of Sexual Harassment.*

To say that the queer grad conferences following this one were somehow less salacious would be to deny the facility that queer studies has always had for riding the pleasure-waves of controversy, and the gatherings to follow most certainly used Gallop's scandalous position as a guerrilla seductress to energize their own discussions of sex and pedagogy. Conferences followed at Champaign-Urbana, the University of Iowa, and finally at Columbia University in 1993, where the day-long "Crossings Over" event for queer grads was sponsored by the now-defunct Lesbian and Gay Studies Group. Sarah Chinn, who presented at "Crossings Over," remembers how "a young man stood up to comment on our discussion on being out as students and teachers. For him the basic problem was not how to speak his sexuality, but how to wear it. His passionate subjectivities—drag queen, gender bender, skirt-wearing-sissy—were literally confined to the closet" (Garber 245).

In 1997, the Center for Lesbian and Gay Studies at the City University of New York held its largest queer graduate conference, "Forms of Desire." The poster for the conference depicts a praying mantis, suggesting both metamorphosis and mimesis, which seem like appropriate tropes for graduate work.[1] Over three days, "Forms" sought to engage with a variety of research fields, and even addressed grads directly: "We at CLAGS are keenly aware of the importance of your work."[2] Panels were diverse, from "Imagined Bodies" to "Queering Comic Books," including talks by advocates from The Audre Lorde Project and New York's Lesbian and Gay Community Services Center. There was even a performance cabaret after the reception. But none of the panels dealt, specifically, with the unique confines of queer *graduate studies*, nor with queer grad student pedagogies. A month before, CLAGS hosted a conference entitled "Queer Pedagogy," which included discussions by Jill Dolan (then ED) and Martin Duberman, but this involved queer faculty rather than graduate pedagogy.[3]

Since 2000, the "Queer-CUNY" conferences, which are affiliated with CLAGS but almost entirely student-organized, have attempted to fill this void, Queer-CUNY I, entitled "Campus Organizing Across the Boroughs,"[4] seemed to take a labor-intensive and activist perspective on queer studies, but offered no panels aimed primarily at grad students. A roundtable session, "On Display," was addressed to "Out Faculty and Staff," which probably included grads, but wasn't designed to take up their particular strategies or concerns. Robert Reid-Pharr, in an issue of the *CUNY Matters* newsletter, mentions it as a forum "to discuss the joys and travails of being out—or not out, or semi-out—on campus" (qtd. in Schmidgall, 11). The second Queer-CUNY conference, in 2001, asked specific questions like "how can our graduates find work in gay and lesbian organizations,"[5] although even this presumed an attitude of optimistic futurity, rather than addressing the concrete needs of queer graduates still involved in M.A. and PhD programs in the present. Unlike "Forms of Desire" in 1997, this 2001 conference included panels on particular "borough campuses" and workshops for student-organizing. Queer-CUNY III, the first titled conference ("Broadening Queer"), began to move in larger theoretical circles, trying to "[explode] our preconceived definitions and categories of gender and sexuality" while simultaneously "amplifying the voices that are too seldom heard."[6] Panels included "an assessment of the climate of . . . [s]afety, events, and queer academia [on] each CUNY campus" that was open to students, faculty, and staff, as well as discussions of "current CUNY-wide student organizing."[7]

Only one document pertaining to "Queer-CUNY IV" exists, a poster[8] outlining that the conference will focus "on LGBTQ students in the classroom" and "LGBTQ pedagogy," but it's unclear if this refers to graduate students, undergrads, or queer faculty. One panel, "Queer in the Classroom," may have taken up all three of these positions, but there is no other extant information on this. Queer-CUNY V, "Celebrating the Global Rainbow," exists only within the online archives of the CLAGS website, although there is a schedule provided. This conference, interestingly, was hosted at LaGuardia Community College rather than at a senior college like Hunter, which seems to be precisely the kind of embattled space that previous events were reaching out to. Rather than having an academic keynote, Queer-CUNY V had Verna Eggleston, Commissioner of New York's Human Resources Administration, who talked about HIV/AIDS and homelessness. Panels included "inter-campus connections," and "Teaching Queer 101"—which, interestingly, did seem aimed at queer graduate instructors—and the reception ended with a dance. I'll talk more about dancing later.

Queer-CUNY VI, "Echoes of Truth Through the Voices of Our Youth," didn't seem to focus precisely on youth at all. I wonder if "youth" referred to undergraduate students, to young graduate students, or to junior faculty. There are no further details, except that the keynote address was given by Alan Van Capelle, Executive Director of Empire State Pride Agenda. Once again, the conference-conveners chose to move away from the standard academic keynote, although the stress placed on Van Capelle's own youth—his status as "one of the youngest LGBT leaders in the nation"—reads suspiciously like the uncritical valorization of young intellectuals. Finally, there is no available information on Queer-CUNY VII, except that it was called "Exploring and Challenging Our Identities." I suspect that precious little administrative attention was paid to this 2006 conference, since CLAGS was invested quite heavily in its own "CLAGS at 15" anniversary celebration and gala.[9] Even though Queer-CUNY VII was only held last year, it already seems to have vanished off the Graduate Center's radar.

This brings us to Queer-CUNY VIII, "The Twilight of Queerness," which I was fortunate enough to have attended quite recently. During the seven years that I spent doing graduate studies at Simon Fraser University in Vancouver, British Columbia—supposedly one of the most queer-friendly cities in the world—I never knew about any queer studies conferences in the area, let alone conferences aimed at queer students. As a result, when I arrived at Queer-CUNY VIII, I was amazed and overwhelmed at the number of young, brilliant, and fiercely beautiful intellectuals around me—crammed into classrooms and hallways, passing out fliers and magazines, conferring about panels, laughing and bitching and networking with each other. I'd never seen anything like it, and I felt, quite suddenly, that I was no longer alone. This was the first conference that I ever attended whose audience members actually engaged one another in productive conversation, not to tear each other down, but to support each other. I expected four or five people to show up to my panel—there were at least thirty people, all listening, all interested. I kept grinning. My colleagues probably thought I'd blown a brain gasket.

Two contributors to this volume—Loren Krywanczyk and Marty Fink—presented with me on a panel devoted to queer pedagogy, with Loren discussing strategies for queering pedagogy in middle-school, and Marty discussing, openly and passionately, her experiences of institutional homophobia while teaching within the CUNY system.[10] For the first time at a conference, I found myself furiously scribbling down notes on every presenter, as well as what audience members were saying. I ran out of paper and started writing down things on my program, then on my conference folder, then on any surface that I could find. The second panel that I attended, called "Local Strategies, Global Resistance," focused on intersections between queer and trans politics at the level of advocacy, and sometimes at street-level. Julian Wolfe, a counsellor at Sylvia's House in New York, spoke with power and concision about homeless queer youth and the role of adult mentoring. When an audience member called him out on his perceived assumptions about homelessness, he admitted that "I used to be homeless too." Swirling topics ranged from the "Rainbow Flags for Momea" organizational movement, to the experience of physically transitioning as an activist within anti-imperialist groups. I looked around, and realized that all of the English grads had gone home. This was not a conversation that you'd hear at a literature conference. I was listening very, very closely, and I was incredibly excited.

I've included this context on queer grad conferences in general—and the Queer-CUNY conferences as a particular case study, on which no work has really been done—in order to figure out what happened to all of the former interest in queer graduate students and their shifting positions within the academy. Apart from Queer-CUNY, there are no annual queer grad forums that I know about. New York, supposedly an epicenter of queer culture, has shut down most of its LGBT resources in the last few years, including bookstores like A Different Light, while Oscar Wilde Books—the last gay bookstore in the city—struggles continually to pay the rent for its West Village building. Where are the NYU and Columbia conferences devoted to queer grads, funded generously by the cash that these private institutions supposedly possess?

Considering that, in 2004, professional union-busters on the Bush-appointed NLRB made it their mission to annihilate NYU's union of graduate and adjunct teachers, it seems as if American private schools still have very little investment in giving basic civil and economic securities to their most overworked and undervalued teachers. Canada, my own country of citizenship, is no better. Contract teaching-faculty at the University of Toronto weren't allowed to unionize under CUPE (Local 3902)[11] until 2003, after a massive 2001 strike, and they continue to push for more (i.e., basic) benefits and representation. Canadian institutions operate on a different system than the US private/public binary, and Buschbaum notes that, despite some victories, "graduate students at private universities represent a relatively new terrain for organizing" (83). Most grads, like other contract faculty, become adept at running between city campuses for very little remuneration; they become, in essence, what Christine Farris calls "'freeway-flyers,' teaching section upon section of composition on multiple campuses, with no hopes of advancement" (19).

My PhD was well-funded by the Social Sciences and Humanities Research Council of Canada, and my graduate institution, like most Canadian schools, didn't allow its students to teach as adjuncts—that is, to teach a course by ourselves—until we were already working on our dissertations. As a result, I spent most of my M.A. and about half of my doctorate as a graduate teaching assistant, which, although a lot of work, is still nothing compared to what most American grads at public universities face in terms of sessional instruction. Most students at the CUNY Graduate Center have to combine federal and private grants with *at least* two sections of adjunct teaching per semester in order to survive in New York. Fellow Canucks who have been lucky enough to secure SSHRC-funding for their stay at the Graduate Center still have to teach for food and rent, since SSHRC, despite its reputation as the grad student lottery, does not make its recipients flush with disposable cash. Combined grants, fellowships, research-assistant jobs (usually death by photocopying), tend to amount to nothing more than a precarious living wage for grad students, who are then pressured to attend expensive, international conferences and buy every *au current* theoretical text in their discipline, all to secure an eventual tenure-track position that most likely doesn't even exist.

What this all has to do with queer grad students, specifically, is a matter of added psychological and financial pressure, both from within departments and, more nebulously, from "outside" by various LGBT communities. It is my belief, culled from personal experience and from endless conversations with other queer grads—a belief simultaneously upheld and challenged by the contributors to this volume—that queer grads are pushed harder by their committees, by their schools, and by the academic culture industry in general. We are encouraged to publish more and faster, to attend more conferences, and to fight more rabidly for our precarious place within the global tenure system, even as, at the same time, we are urged to divorce our sexuality from our academic work in subtle, pernicious, and soul-destroying ways. Queer grads are pushed harder because our queerness is often seen as a transformative kind of disability, a physical and cultural stigma whose power flows both ways, a crippling agency. Our sexuality allows us to participate in some of the most exciting theory-production and meaning-making within the academy, but it also marks us as "narrow" candidates on the job market, as academics *only interested* in sexuality, as queer inmates within a pedagogical prison that could keep us from getting that treasured, imagined job.

So we are pushed towards excellence, towards that fiction of academic rigor, which often translates absurdly as knowing everything about everything that every university cares about, being able to teach everything about everything while simultaneously appearing focused, categorizable, replicable as a cultural laborer on that most precious of identification papers, the CV. Why doesn't the CV have a picture when every other recognizable ID document does? Why don't we simply declare our gender/sex on our CV, as we are forced to do on our driver's license? Because, make no mistake about it: committees are curious. They want to know, *is this candidate for our queer studies position* actually, measurably, categorically, *queer*? Queer for real? LGBT grad students are often trapped in an impossible binary, which really hasn't changed since the early 1990s when the most books (2) were published on academic homophobia: do they pass as straight and risk not showing enough passion for the job ("I'm just crazy-in-love with composition studies!"), or do they try to teach what they love—teach about whom and why they love—and risk never getting that coveted joint-appointment in English and Women's Studies?

Is being queer worth being poor? Is it worth passing up a $50,000/month job that happens to be in North Carolina? Is it worth constantly being told by your supervisory committees that you should "really just focus on reading for your field exams," while you're trying to organize queer poetry readings on campus? Is it worth having to come out every minute of every day, again and again, until you feel stripped naked, whipped and slapped, at every meeting, every conference, every dinner—until your sexuality becomes a swollen, badly-stitched wound that you have to rip open again and again, saying, "See, I'm still a fag/dyke/transboy/girl, isn't that odd?" This disclosure occurs in opposition to the normally transparent and invisible body of the professor, a reality echoed by bell hooks when she observes, in *Teaching To Transgress*: "Trying to remember the bodies of my professors, I find myself unable to recall them. I hear voices, remember fragmented ideas, but very few whole bodies" (192). Martha Holmes, in her edited volume *The Teacher's Body*, admits that "student bodies often command most of the attention in college classrooms. Young or old, pierced or tattooed, sleeping or rapt, these bodies dominate the room and seem to justify its existence." The body of the teacher, however, can be "both present and irrelevent"[12] (7), a fact that holds up when we think of all the popular teen TV shows with absent or invisible teachers. The role of queer teachers may be to explode this image, to *inhabit*, as it were, a classroom, even as we are accused constantly of inhabiting that space *too queerly*. So how can we productively materialize ourselves as physical beings in the classroom, and how positive a gesture is this?

We might ask the same thing of contemporary queer theory, which often requires separate doctoral degrees in film and cultural studies in order to translate, especially for grad students who might just be starting their M.A. degrees and encountering writers like Judith Butler and Michele Foucault for the first time. How do we materialize queer theory, make it "appear," for new readers and instructors? What is queer theory worth? Have queer grads somehow become absorbed into this complex theoretical enterprise, so that they live and breathe and fluoresce and smell like queer theory, so that they become living holograms of queer poststructuralism? James Penney, in "(Queer) Theory and the Universal Alternative," notes critically that "One has been hard-put since the emergence of so-called 'queer theory' to find an authentically radical socialist voice," and rightly accuses the theoretical project of having a "Foucauldian narcissistic inwardness that severs the imagination" (3; 6).

Like Timothy Brennan, who often levels searing critiques at those political academics he perceives to be neoliberal or "cosmopolitan," Penney isn't afraid to critique his own theoretical homestead; however, his argument fails to factor in the wealth of incredibly ethical and socially engaged criticism being done within global queer theories, such as the writing of Sarah Ahmed, Kevin Kumashiro, Robert Reid-Pharr, and Chandra Mohanty, just to name a few. Still, this indictment of queer theory as a sometimes "narcissistic" and apolitical discipline, often engaged in the most exquisitely complicated theoretical embroidery, is necessary and valid. When Kumashiro, in *Troubling Education*, demands of one of his interviewees (a lesbian middle-school teacher), "Why aren't you involved in working against other forms of oppression?" (196), the question at first seems hostile, but then makes a lot of sense.

What, then, is being queer worth to queer grads? And how do we rescue queerness from this oppressive value-system when we can't rescue our own bodies from it, when we can't leap out of the way of the speeding truck because we've actually made our homes and our lives on the freeway, as "freeway flyers?"

I am writing this introduction while on a bus from Toronto to New York, surrounded by perfectly sensible people who, unlike me, have managed to fall asleep despite, or because, of the coach's rhythmic rocking back and forth as it crosses numerous borders ideological and concrete, visible and occult. To be a graduate student is to be constantly in transition, perpetually translated, always en route to a further and yet-to-be-imagined institutional homestead, which is also theoretically similar to being queer. As I hope to discuss within this introduction, graduate students within and across the humanities form a singular type of laboring strata, a particular model of surplus production that can be audaciously sutured into the uneven terrain of Marx's commodity fetish. There are multiple exploited workforces whose non-reciprocal labor helps to iron out the contradictions in late capitalism, and graduate students in the humanities act as *part* of this solution[13] within the labor-sphere of the university. Privileged, empowered, funded, armed with a toolbox of powerful heuristic devices—but still concretely exploited as non-tenured, replicable, and imprintable labor.

And part of that experience, of my particular experience, can be articulated solely through the valences of marginality that I occupied during that time and continue to occupy now. These include: queerness, mental and financial instability, illness, exhaustion, and loneliness. Many of these represent common positions that are forced upon graduate students, or, paradoxically, critical spaces of reflection and resistance, life-modes taken on *in defiance* of institutional apathy and discrimination against creative thought. What seem on the surface to be disabling trajectories can, through grace, valor, and flexibility, become tactics for survival, even prosperity. As someone who identifies keenly yet uncertainly with experiences of concrete disability—as someone with scars, missing and/or "improperly" fashioned body parts, internal as well as external glitches and entanglements—my identifications with "queerness" and "disability" are always mediated by my facility to pass as nondisabled and nonqueer. My marks are mostly on the inside. But, in this sense, I feel that I can only study gender and sexuality as embodiments or utterances along a continuum of dis/ability and acceptable bodily comportment and texture, as scars that cross each other on a dermal plane.

As an infant, born two months premature, I was given a 10 percent chance of survival; my fraternal twin was not so lucky. Now I am all about screwing with the odds. And, given that 10 to 20 percent probably also represents the average graduate student's chance of scoring a desirable tenure-track job—in their area, with proper pay and benefits, near a place they want to live, at a school where they're excited and even proud to teach—I can only think that the best possible resistance to the oppressive inequalities of the tenure system is to ignore the percentile and apply anyways, or even to apply for what you seem least likely to get. Take a job without the intention of making tenure.

This volume is about a range of queer embodied voices—bodies and voices that have insisted not upon representation, or even performance, but rather upon the materialization of an imbalanced and improper equation: the recognition of partiality and partiality of recognition. All of the contributors have been encouraged to write from perspectives of emotional and erotic particularity rather than strategic and analogue criticality, the "non-I" of supposedly marketable scholarly writing. Each author has chosen to delineate their own subjective queer "moments" within traditional, policed, or even openly hostile academic systems and localities. Many have endeavored to express the concrete resistances they faced both during and after taking on certain projects, pedagogies, readings, and orientations. This reportage is meant not as some kind of institutional betrayal, but much more productively as a critical *report* on the binding (and sometimes blinding) relationships between queerness, pedagogy, and *service*. Graduate students are supposed to perform a variety of educational and diacritical "services" to their department, and in return, that department and its administrators must provide them with a reciprocal fostering service, a tricky combination of nurturance, critical expression, and professionalization. Such reciprocity is not always evident.

Queer grads, this volume argues, occupy a uniquely shifting terrain among other junior and non-tenured intellectuals, teachers-in-training, and writers, and that tenuous balance emerges from a kaleidoscopic sense of differential marginalities that risk being silently and lucratively absorbed into departments that feed on difference. Queer grads are often given the impression by "forward-thinking" institutions that their sexuality, their physical embodiment, and their localized histories of oppression are not worth commenting on, not at issue, not the sum total of their academic life. Or, on the opposite end of the spectrum, they are told that queerness is very much of the moment, very fundable, very popular, even as their classroom experiences do not match up with these optimistic and facile sentiments; even as their attempts to grapple with bodily and experiential knowledges and narratives are discouraged in favor of the uncritical memorization and recapitulation of decontextualized theoretical traditions—what bell hooks calls the "banking" model of scholarly acquisition. In *Teaching to Transgress*, she describes almost perfectly my first experience of reading feminist-psychoanalytic criticism in a graduate seminar:

> Of what use is feminist theory that literally beats [students] down, leaves them stumbling bleary-eyed from classroom settings feeling humiliated, feeling as though they could easily be standing in a living room or bedroom somewhere naked with someone who has seduced them or is going to, who also subjects them to a process of interaction that humiliates, that strips them of their sense of value? (65).

Here, hooks is talking particularly about the experience of female students coming to theory for the first time, the same theory that Gloria Watkins, as a graduate student, once came to "as a location for healing." As this volume explores, many graduate students who identify (or refuse to identify) along a spectrum of LGBTQ modalities have also come to theory looking for a balm, a cipher, a Kevlar vest, a weapon, a calculus, or a second skin. Many are disappointed, not only by homo- and trans-phobia within the western deconstructionist tradition, but by the perplexing absences of queer-materialist, global-feminist, and radical revolutionary critiques within graduate seminars. Chela Sandoval, in *Methodology of the Oppressed*, identifies what she calls a "dangerous state of theoretical apartheid" within the academy, noting a "shotgun arrangement" (41; 61) between hegemonic theory (including queer theory) on the one hand and global/Third-World feminisms on the other. Many students, despite the best efforts of caring and politically engaged faculty, admit to the experience of feeling lost and alone within the crystalline structures of theoretical inquiry, unable to see themselves reflected in the bewildering array of surfaces that are offered *en masse* in an effort to fulfill arcane requirements of scholastic breadth (canon) and perceived humanistic "rigor" (i.e., eligible for qualifying exams, which merely replicate this empty category of rigor/mortis).

I like to ask why things are queer—what makes something queer, how does it sign queerly, how does it enact a queer verb or what Foucault would call a queer "style of life/*mode da vie*?" Many critics have asked, and continue to ask, what is queer about a variety of literary forms. Some have asked what is queer about theory, what is queer about resistance, what isn't, what might be. Rather than asking what is "queer" about being a graduate student, this volume asks how a broad spectrum of graduate students have chosen to enact and maintain queer positions within their respective institutions, against a constellation of (perhaps) unexpected hostilities, and in the face of a political pluralism which tells them how exceptional and ordinary they are at the same time for being queer intellectuals. Does queerness graduate? Can it be revised, marked, and defended within different institutional settings? Can it pass or fail? Can it negotiate a new contract, or go on strike? Can it get a term-long extension?

How are queer students also, in some way, students of queerness? And when we graduate, do we lose our liminality, which may have both constrained and rewarded us? I felt nothing upon graduating. Nothing but fear.

This discussion provides the chance to conjoin and enact a number of evocative pairings and binaries that impact the lives and careers of queer graduate students. We come out daily, in a sense, as many different *citizens*: as erotic subjects who go against the grain, as bodies difficult to class, as students who are also teachers, as teachers who make very little money, as recipients of federal and provincial/state funding and simultaneously as debtors within the transnational student loan system, as privileged culture-eaters, as "drains" on "*your* tax dollars," as retail failures, as social misanthropes, as topics of familial embarrassment, and finally as professional non-citizens who often must straddle international borders with little or no medical insurance in order to move through intellectual spaces that have been fashioned and are now strictly regulated by the wealthy academic elite, the lords and ladies of the lecture circuit. I've heard rumors that one particularly well-known and celebrated intellectual has grad students pick up dry cleaning in an effort to compete for precious time and favor. Like Kenneth Anger, I'm not immune to a good scandal. Many queer graduate students, like queer and trans folk across the world, have developed faculties of critical camp and irony as a tactic for energizing joy and fellowship within social arenas that daily seek their cultural erasure.

In my first semester of grad school, I invited a professor to join me—along with a group of classmates—for coffee in the cafeteria. Instead, I was given $1 to *bring* the professor a cup of coffee, and furthermore told to return with change, as if there might be any. This was one of my first crucial lessons in academic hierarchy. Later, the same professor informed me, along with another classmate, that our demeanor in seminar had been "unprofessional,"[14] chiefly because we were usually in a good mood and didn't take a lot of notes. I would soon learn that note-taking was also notation, the fixing of a particular kind of student identity—head bowed, eyes down, hand on the page—which Eve Sedgwick identifies as the posture of shame; the posture of reading.[15] I would argue that graduate students are often driven to read shamefully, or to read-in-shame, woundedly and silently receiving knowledge, when in fact they need to be given the space to *read* shame as a marvelous tension between inside and outside, a reading-template given to them (sometimes unconsciously) by faculty, whose margins are only legible if they can be viewed from a distance.

When I first started to meet other queer graduate students—often at conferences, or in other alienating and temporary settings—we would almost always share similar stories of isolation within our respective departments, anger at the lack of courses on sexual diversity, or the mad hope that *next year* some more folks like us might arrive in a new cohort. Inevitably, the conference would end, and we would go back home, keeping in contact via email and sporadically complaining to each other about problems of agency and access. What surprised me most was that grad students attending culturally powerful and visibly wealthy schools—some of the most privileged cultural spaces in the western world—were often the ones who complained most stridently about a lack of queer resources. Often, it was the rural and isolated schools that developed new and inventive forms of queer kinship and advocacy, while the famous and funded institutions maintained a near-perfect adherence to the canonicity and patriarchal tradition that had made them powerful in the first place.

As a grad student, I was shocked at how unwelcome I felt in my university's LGBT space. This was through no fault of its incredibly hardworking coordinators, but rather the result of its inevitable fragmentation as an "inclusive" space that was mostly inhabited by gay white men. I asked one of the coordinators if other graduate students or professors volunteered their time, and was told that queer faculty on the whole had little contact with any type of queer student advocacy on campus. There was a list of LGBT faculty, but one had to—through the logic of tautology—be faculty in order to access the list. So, even if we had allies, we were prevented from contacting them by multiple frames of security.

One often had to play a delicate guessing game. What did "gender studies" mean on a professor's profile? What were the secret ciphers, the colored handkerchiefs, and did they signify what we thought they did? Just as a misreading on the dancefloor (or in the darkness of the pub) might earn you an awkward surprise in the bedroom, our tactical readings of professors' emotional and theoretical investments could backfire on us in the classroom. Assigning excerpts from *Bodies That Matter* didn't necessarily render someone queer-positive, and even openly gay faculty could be witheringly critical, dismissive, even hostile about sexually experimental work. Assurances of "you need to be *more than just* queer on your CV" became acidly legible to me for what they really suggested: our lives and our loves were not enough, would not be enough, to guarantee a position within the competitive global tenure system.

In her 2007 article "Wittig's Material Practice,"[16] Judith Butler gets personal about her days as a graduate student. This is surprising, since, unlike her forerunner Eve Sedgwick—whose work has always taken staunch pleasure in being personal—Butler has tended to maintain a surface of exquisite professionalism within her discussions of sexuality and the rhetoric of gender. It was not until her 2001 article, "Doing Justice to Somebody"—wherein, speaking of intersexuality and the John/Joan case, she asks with unvarnished anger "is femininity properly embodied here? Is the embodiment working? Is it? Is it? How do we know?" (629)—that I began to see a distinctly personal, even antagonistic vein emerging within Butler's later writing. This gave me hope that some of the critical rage and immediacy of late-1980s queer theory, particularly AIDS writing, was beginning once again to suppurate and bleed within what had become the largely antipersonal and theoretically amplified canon of queer theory post-1990. Speaking of Monique Wittig's notion that lesbian lovers must "take each other apart," literally dismember and rearticulate each other, through the act of queer desire, Butler is concerned in this article with conjoining the seemingly politically exclusive concepts of "lesbian" and "universality" as a radical form of queer rhetoric. Indeed, what if the lesbian position were the "universal one," and everything we knew about love, sex, and desire had to emerge from a type of global lesbian perspective? "A lesbian's life," Butler posits, "[could] be a figure for life itself, her desire a figure for desire itself" (525).

What comes, for me, as the biggest surprise in this article is when Butler—so feared among queer and straight grad students alike as the fashioner of sharply professional, cryptic, and sometimes exhausting theoretical writing—begins to talk clearly and personally about her experience as a grad student at Yale. She speaks of the Simone de Beauvoir conference in 1979 as "the first conference I ever attended . . . [I] had just graduated from college. I did not know where I was" (528). This reminded me of the first conference I attended as an M.A. student, called "Transculturalisms," during which I and my peers were followed by security, reprimanded for eating food that "didn't belong to us" (we were starving), and repeatedly asked who we were, what school we came from, and *did we belong* there? During an incredibly solemn presentation on avant-garde Canadian cinema, my friend Nancy had to run out of the hall (or rather clomp out in her excellent military surplus boots) because she couldn't stop laughing, in the same way that you might laugh uncontrollably at a funeral.

Butler talks about attending one of the first queer events at Yale, and I can feel her awkward, honest trepidation as a not-entirely-out graduate student trying to determine what various strata she might come to occupy within Yale's deep catacombs of power and privilege. In speaking of attending a demonstration in front of the library, that institutional bastion of genderless and de-sexed "knowledge," her tone moves warmly from suspicion, to candor, to a kind of joy:

> there was [the] first gay pride day on the Yale campus, and a number of us (who were "we"?) met to stand with our signs and publicly declared ourselves in front of Sterling Library. This was not easy for me. I was a philosophy major and frequenting Hegel and Kant seminars at the same time . . . [S]uddenly the music was louder, and we all started, at first quite awkwardly, to dance. Even now, I cannot quite imagine myself having done it (529).

It's hard for me to imagine one of my favorite writers dancing. We know it happens, but the actual event is hard to picture. Yet try to picture, just for a moment, the scene of theorists dancing; the scene of theoretical dance, of meaning-making as performance. Judith Butler spinning Jack Halberstam around in a queer foxtrot as big band music plays in the background. Lee Edelman and Douglas Crimp slow-dancing, head on shoulder, hands clasped, grinning ruefully as Cole Porter begins the beguine.

The new kids—Ian Aeng, Claire Hemmings, Peter Dickinson, Helen Leung, Robert Reid-Pharr, Jay Prosser—dancing to mash-up beats and drinking cheap high-balls. Look out, Robert McCruer is drunk again, and Jose Munoz just showed up with Vivian Namaste, who's handing out glow-sticks.

Petra Kuppers is gliding in her chair, decorating everyone with ribbon and lights and streamers that burn in the dark. Chip Delany is not to be trusted at the bar.

Then there are the baby queer theorists—us—leaning against the bleachers and watching the whole scene unfold, full of wonder. Eve Sedgwick checks on us to make sure that we've all got rides home, then goes back to doing the hustle with Larry Kramer, even letting him wear her white glasses. And above and below and around us all, like Donne's "gold to airy thinness beat," or the touch of invisible sequins, the fabulous spectral presence of those now gone: Michael Lynch, Jacques Derrida, Susan Sontag, Pepper LaBeija, Paul Monette, Dorian Corey, Kathy Acker, Brandon Teena, Matt Shepard, Billy Gautier, David Wojnarowicz, Keith Harring, Andy Warhol. Why invoke their names? Because names are a sacred calculus, and we are *their* guests at this event.

Imagine rapture. Rainbow lights signifying a perversity of polysemic investments and energies: queerness, diffraction, pulsation, myth, precocity, childhood, coloring books, Christmas, liminality; and, most unavoidably, sexuality as an effect of two or three or multiple colliding weather-systems, the mist and light and coruscation of liquid and air, hot and cold, visible and ultraviolet. Imagine a dance palace with neon fish-tanks, full of rainbow-colored tetras and day-glow oceanic furniture, treasure chests spilling out gold, pearls, and lapidary. Imagine Elmer's Glue, glitter, construction paper in an inexhaustible supply of colors, tissue streamers, garlands, and overstuffed couches where Jeanette Winterson and Nicole Brossard recline, reading poetry inscribed on chains of glass that only further amplify and reflect the dizzying, polymorphous light; and the glow of the false constellations as they move overhead, from the piece of Grand Central Station's ceiling that we stole and then suspended with a mess of golden wire, fiber-optic cable, flexible pipe-cleaners, shoe-laces, gum, amylase, and duct tape. Like Belize's version of Heaven in Kushner's *Angels in America*, with dragons, clubs, and voting booths on every corner. And the library is just one massive, neverending shelf with the call number HQ 76.5, expanding in all directions.

Or maybe this isn't what we want. Maybe it's stupid, facile, and utopic, a lonely kid's dream of what fellowship might look like. Maybe, as queer academics, we do better and more responsible work when we're stuck in tiny adjunct offices, dehydrated from coffee and sick from cigarettes, filling out endless mechanical interlibrary loan forms because our libraries never seem to have the books we need (I imagine that, somewhere underground or maybe floating in a bubble underwater, there is a central clearing-house library for queer materials that simply has everything). If the libraries that I've had access to had given as much attention to queer, feminist-materialist, and pedagogical texts as they did to introductory science textbooks—often inexplicably accumulating from the 1950s onwards and clogging every shelf with their weirdly fetishistic geometric covers—then I would have been able to spend more time *exploring* the library and less time clicking the "submit form" button from my home computer. The Queer Collective at Simon Fraser University, run almost entirely by student volunteers, still has a better LGBT book selection than the seven-floor campus library.

It's pointless, even anti-productive, to sit back and anticipate an eventual gender/sex paradise whose very existence will eliminate all the critical thought and resistance that historically made such a state possible in the first place. But that doesn't mean that we can't have a little more fun as students and teachers, and that we can't locate radical transformation within the very acts of laughing, dancing, smiling, joking, and winking from across battle-lines. Affect can attach marvelously to different objects in different ways, and we can't ever retrace its circumlocutions and arrive at the same design. Anger can spark mirth, desolation can produce erotics, and intensity—even "rigor"—can sometimes lead to play for its own sake.

What I'm suggesting here is not that overworked grad students should all slip on their tank tops and go dancing, but that we should acknowledge dancing as a possibility for theoretical liberation, as a form of queer choreography. All graduation ceremonies are performative events that enshrine precise musical, fashionable (in the literal sense of color-coded vestments), and dramatic codes, and grad students are always somehow interpolated by the liminality of graduation as an *event*. But how should we comport ourselves when we walk toward the stage? And why walk at all? Our bodies can be queer syllabi. Our bodies constantly interact with interlaced fields of magnetic and quantum energy, and most academics who study performance genres will admit to believing in a kind of dramatic aura, a *kinesphere*, that structures, propels, and galvanizes movement on the stage, so that some small gesture from a dancer in the wings can have an enormous kinematic effect on someone standing at the center. We teach with our limbs, and these have a unique and powerful history of being choreographed against multiple valences of oppression, as a singular bodily song. It is time then, I think, for post-millennial queer theory to start seriously dancing its ass off, especially if we're to combat the seditious and casual ways in which academic professionalization keeps us from dancing at all.

There should be more dancing, more joy, even more fucking ABBA. Queer grads, faculty, and allies should be encouraged to work together, to foster each other's continuing work, to reproduce new and fabulous and dangerous species of queerness rather than recapitulating the same formal essays and theoretical traditions in order to cohere a reputation as professional proofreaders. When Jane Gallop kissed her graduate student on the lips, she may not have fully known the pedagogical value (and violence) of this action, but it still maintains a kind of productive resistance, a savage joy. Gallop sought to rematerialize the queer teacher's absent body, and, with this volume, I (we) hope to once again outline and rematerialize the bodies of queer grad students—bodies upon which the double-edged inscriptitory energies of the academy have acted sometimes cruelly, sometimes fatally.

If we are indeed the queer babes of the academy, the progeny of millennial sexual cultures and poststructuralist powers, then our goal should be to emerge wailing and angry like all survivalist infants, shaking our little fists and pissing all over the startled hands of our interlocutors. Our comprehensive exams should be as pornographic as possible, our theses and dissertations gift-wrapped sparkling bombs, our conference presentations loud, profane, and requiring security to escort us across the street. We should all be assholes, because being an asshole is sometimes the only proper pedagogy left when you're trying to save lives.

Hence, the existence of this volume—as a text representing the newest and most fascinating work done by queer graduate students, and also as a capsule of the experiences of resistance, homophobia, transphobia, silencing, and betrayal that these students have seen/felt on their way to where they are now. These essays deal with a panoply of queer topics, including: transitioning while teaching, how/why to teach queer theory, guerilla pedagogy, bisexuality and theory, queer life-writing, police and administrative brutality, institutional homophobia, urban and rural queer dichotomies, the challenges of the global tenure system, the intersections of academia/advocacy, and the many possible futures of queer graduate students and allies within the academy. Just as I was overwhelmed by the presence at Queer-CUNY VIII, I am also shocked, awed, and filled with energizing hope and joy by the amazing contributors to this volume. It is my honor and privilege to provide a forum for their stories, their theories, and their protests.

NOTES

1. April 3–5, 1997 "Forms of Desire" program, Courtesy of CLAGS.
2. Ibid, page 1, "Welcome."
3. Archived CLAGS event schedule, "Queer Pedagogy Conference," March 8, 1997.
4. Poster, "Campus Organizing Across the Boroughs," May 6, 2000.
5. Poster, "2nd Annual Queer-CUNY Conference," March 10, 2001.
6. Poster, "Broadening Queer: The 3rd Annual Queer-CUNY Conference," April 19, 2002.
7. Program, "Broadening Queer," April 19, 2002.
8. Poster, "Building Bridges," April 5, 2003.

9. It is certainly not my attention to criticize CLAGS here, which deserves as many gala celebrations as it can get, and whose crucial mission has always been "to promote new and disseminate existing scholarship . . . on gay and lesbian lives" (CLAGS Bylaws 1). As I was looking through records in the CLAGS office, I found correspondence going back to the early-1990s indicating that CLAGS has always fought for the fair distribution of its endowment funds, with Executive Directors having to contend with unbearable condescension from financial departments at CUNY (who are always seemingly astonished when CLAGS wants to allocate its own money). The Kessler and Rockefeller Endowments, in particular, have in the past been mishandled, with quizzical interest statements being made available to CLAGS staff only after the financial quarter in question was done (Email: Nov 30, 2001; Financial Document, July 3, 2001), or interest not accumulating in proper coincidence with the market. This problem emerges from CUNY's attempts as an over-extended institution to patch its own financial problems, rather than at the level of CLAGS, which is run remarkably given its small staff and lack of resources.

10. Fink notes that she was reprimanded for being "too queer" in the classroom, despite the fact that her students overwhelmingly enjoyed her discussions of writers like James Baldwin and Audre Lorde. She was told by an administrator that she "had an axe to grind," i.e., that she was pushing a queer political agenda on her students, which leads us to believe that queer teachers somehow emanate or signal queerness through their very bodily presence within the classroom.

11. York University in Toronto recently added an accessible fund for its trans-identified students, built into its union local, that workers can apply for (a situation that would certainly result in decertification at NYU).

12. In *Troubling Education*, Kevin Kumashiro interviews a lesbian middle-school teacher, Sam, who asks this question succinctly by echoing the questions of her students: "Where do teachers live? In a broom closet? You know, do they just, like, float, suspended? Or do they really feel?" (29).

13. In *Outside In the Teaching Machine*, Gayatri Spivak notes that "necessary practicalities"—i.e, "what are the best available textbooks" and how can this be "integrated into the English curriculum without disturbing the distribution requirements?"—often result in a pedagogical situation wherein these concerns "become tacitly accepted rules for the [course] planners, [and] the recipients (students, audiences) often think of pedagogy as only consciousness transformation" (62). Her analysis, though astute, does not factor in the liminal and often doubly-marginalized role of graduate students who are simultaneously audiences, students, and instructors.

14. In *Teaching Community*, bell hooks notes "[the] many times I was told, and read in my files, that I did not have the 'proper demeanor of a graduate student,' which meant that I dared to challenge my professors and refused to accept passively their domination" (88).

15. In *Shame and its Sisters*, Sedgwick notes that "if, as Tomkins describes it, the lowering of the eyelids, the lowering of the eyes, the hanging of the head is the attitude of shame, it may also be that of reading" (28).

16. My fellow panellist, Seth Clark Silberman, also has an essay on Wittig (from which his conference paper was drawn) in this issue of GLQ: the splendidly titled "I Have Access To Your Glottis."

BIBLIOGRAPHY

Butler, Judith. "Wittig's Material Practice." *GLQ* 13.1 (2007): 519–33.

———. "Doing Justice to Someone." *GLQ* 7.4 (2001): 621–36.

Farris, Christine. *Under Construction: Working at the Intersections of Composition Theory, Research, and Practice*. Logan, UT: Utah State University Press, 1998.

Garber, Linda, ed. *Tilting the Tower: Lesbians/Teaching/Queer Subjects*. New York: Routledge, 1994.

Holmes, Martha. *The Teacher's Body*. SUNY, 2003.

hooks, bell. *Teaching To Transgress*. New York: Routledge, 1994.

———. *Teaching Community*. New York: Routledge, 2003.

Kumashiro, Kevin. *Troubling Education*. New York: Routledge, 2002.

Sandoval, Chela. *Methodology of the Oppressed*. University of Minnesota, 2000.

Schmidgall, Gary. "Center for Lesbian and Gay Studies Parades into Second Decade." *CUNY Matters* Summer 2003: 10–11.

Sedgwick, Eve. *Shame and its Sisters*. Durham, NC: Duke University, 1995.

Spivak, Gayatri. *Outside in the Teaching Machine*. New York: Routledge, 1993.

PART I

1

There Are Transsexuals in Our Middle Schools!

Loren Krywanzcyk

INTRODUCTION

What does it mean to queer pedagogy in the context of an under-resourced public middle school in Brooklyn at a time when queer and trans identities are themselves so controversial in the United States? And what does it mean for me, Mr. Krywanczyk, to attempt to employ queer pedagogical methodologies in my sixth grade English classroom?

These questions are not about or driven by fear, although the main threads of this paper may seem to conjure and symbolize fear. The first of these threads concerns the Panopticon, intimidating Big Brother figure at the center of Michel Foucault's "Discipline and Punish." The second thread concerns Lawrence King, a visibly gender non-conforming, queer eighth grade student shot to death by a fellow student in the computer lab of their California public middle school in February of 2008.

I am slightly wary of foregrounding LGBTQ youth of color in urban public schools, such as King, in a paper for an elite gathering of academics. I aim to bear in mind the materiality of King's body in the context of a public institution without spectacularizing King's death or employing it as a purely negative symbol of the terrifying reality of transphobic violence. After all, Lawrence King attended a public middle school that could be described as similar to the school where I have taught the past three years; and King's identity and self-expression could be described as somewhat similar to that of several sixth grade students whom I have taught.

There is a palpable tension generated by the authority bestowed upon my white, male, Yale-educated body in a classroom space overcrowded with sixth grade students of diverse—though almost entirely non-white—racial identities, almost all of whom receive government subsidized lunches. My transition from being Ms. Krywanczyk my first two years at this school to being Mr. Krywanczyk this year—which seventh and eighth grade students and faculty are aware of, but which most of my sixth graders remain unaware of—heightens and complicates this tension in a manner that only a queer pedagogical approach can effectively address.

INSTITUTIONALIZED INTELLECTUAL VIOLENCE

Public schools like mine funnel young bodies of color into "the system"—juvenile detention facilities, foster care systems, youth prisons—at an alarming rate. Decades ago, Foucault delineated the very kinds of body policing I witness on a daily basis in the hallways of my school. But instead of sitting at a seminar debating the intricacies of Foucault's argument with fellow undergraduates, I now find myself (technically) on the Panopticon's team. My job entails socializing young bodies and minds, a task that carries the power to liberate, oppress, or both. Part of this socialization process, my employers at the Department of Education tell me, involves demanding that youth remove their hats and spit out their gum and face forward when they form two gender-segregated lines. I am supposed to state that "we was" is grammatically incorrect; and that it is, always has been, and always should be "we were."

Radical educators find and create any opportunities we can for small-scale rebellion: "Forget the boys and girls lines! Chew gum if you want in my room, as long as it doesn't end up under my desks!" I listen to Lisa Delpit more carefully than I do my principal—with whom I employ the same "smile and nod" technique my students try to pull off to appease me—and teach lessons about the values of code-switching. I create behavioral contracts between me, Mr. Krywanczyk, and my students. We strategically and thoughtfully break school rules, together. But I remain in the driver's seat in this contractual agreement. And it is far more difficult to break the cycle of intellectual violence that stems from mandates like No Child Left Behind, which places so much emphasis on annual standardized tests that under-resourced schools are pushed to extremes in "teaching to the test."

The shutting down of interactive discourse and critical, non-regurgitative thought that results from this "teaching to the test" has devastating ramifications—particularly on certain (underprivileged) students in certain (underprivileged) schools. In a New York City school system that is appallingly segregated and unequal, the distinctions between students who are encouraged to think critically and create knowledge and students who are applauded when they form a straight line in the hallway (and who are functionally prepared to play a limited role, and nothing more, in a broader capitalist economy) fall consistently along racial and socioeconomic lines.

QUEERING PEDAGOGY

Queer pedagogy combats this prevalent discouragement of critical thought. In queering, there is no closing—and arguably, there is never closure. To queer is to venture into controversial, intellectually complicated, nuanced terrain with students. It requires faith that middle school students in a public school such as mine not only can, but must, learn to grapple with complexity if their education is going to provide opportunities, rather than impose insurmountable limitations.

Queer theory and radical educational theory inform queer pedagogy. Since the 1980s, queer theorists have challenged notions of essential identity categories (and have thereby challenged notions of difference) while simultaneously affirming the distinctions in lived experiences among individuals with different identities. These thinkers recognize that identities overlap in complex ways and they have navigated between a poststructuralist challenge of categorical distinctions—all genders are socially constructed—and a social-justice-driven recognition of the valence of identities in everyday life—Lawrence King was murdered for deviating from social norms of sexuality and gender expression. Attempts to queer are simultaneously crucial and impossible to finish; therefore educators who introduce a queer criticality into our pedagogies have no static or unifying goal to achieve, and we must continually shift our applications of queer pedagogical ideals to the specific physical spaces of our classrooms.

THE LIMITS OF AN "LGBT APPROACH"

A straightforward LGBT approach to gender and sexuality issues in public schools offers a mere BAND-AID solution to bullying, homophobia, and transphobia. Such an approach frames me, Mr. Krywanczyk, as the authority or expert who needs to impart concrete knowledge about identities to students who do not yet know such things. This approach to pedagogy is faulty for a number of reasons, including the fact that queer and trans issues are already realities for my students—in their neighborhoods, families, social lives, and even in themselves. (I will mention but not delve into the racism driving many administrators and faculty members at my school to discourage teachers from even mentioning queer or trans identities. "You know how those Latino/Asian/Black families are" is a phrase that I have heard uttered more than once by white colleagues.) A queer methodology, on the other hand, encourages criticality and considers inquiries about identity as crucial to the act of teaching, rather than material to be covered on one particular day and checked off a "to do" list. In a middle school English classroom, queer pedagogy pushes conversations about characters and identity beyond simplistic observations and into an exploration of power dynamics, social issues arising in texts, and character experience.

WHAT DOES QUEER PEDAGOGY LOOK LIKE IN MR. KRYWANCZYK'S ROOM?

Appealing to difference in a non-tokenizing manner in a middle school classroom requires digging deep into issues of gender, race, and class, and pushing students beyond easy notions of black and white or rich and poor and into a realm of ever-shifting intersections of identity. Middle school students are not only ready to examine complex and sophisticated issues of identity but are already forced to tackle them on their own, if nowhere but in the hallways of our school. Racial typing and stereotyping, sexual harassment, and queer-bashing can be witnessed outside my classroom every day (and this phenomenon is absolutely not specific to under-resourced schools).

When I have most successfully incorporated queer methodologies into my teaching practice, I have deliberately considered three facets of my teaching: my decisions about and execution of academic curricula; my body as a site or channel of various forces and perspectives; and the way in which I establish and foster my classroom environment. I read aloud to my classes Jacqueline Woodson's *From the Notebooks of Melanin Sun,* a phenomenal novel about a 14-year-old biracial boy whose mother comes out to him not only as "queer" (her term of choice) but as in love with a white woman. Student inquiry about this text directs my lessons, which has prompted full-class debates about when, if ever, the words "fag," "dyke," and "queer" should be used, and by whom. Instead of brushing off words like "gay" or "faggot" with hasty or offhand reprimands of "don't say that word!," I try to prevent bullying while encouraging analysis of the varying meanings of these words—literally, historically, and colloquially—just as I would do in studies of other words students stumble across in texts. I shared a news article about Lawrence King's murder with my students last year and posed questions about the decision to try thirteen-year-old shooter Brandon McInerney as an adult and about the politics of hate crime legislation. I received admonishment and complaints from administrators and some colleagues who claimed that I should "be careful, this is awfully mature for sixth graders!" But we can't truly address bullying without closely examining the language that fuels it.

There are, admittedly, dangers of "going there" in such a way with students. Exuding confidence as a transsexual with the seventh and eighth graders in my school is important to me—but there are limits to the subversive or radical potential of being an LGBTQ role model to people at my school, in part because I can in no way be representative of "trans experience." In addition, with each and every class I have struggled to negotiate between skills that will truly open doors for students and those which will appear on standardized tests in January. Where is there any space for explorations of identity—my own, characters', or students'—when many of my students regularly misspell the word "does"? But these thoughts lend themselves to incremental thinking, which is the exact trap that New York politicians fell into when they abandoned trans people in the ENDA push and refused to pass the Dignity for All Students Act. Queering pedagogy in a radical way entails opening, and never shutting down, discourse—even when it is very challenging or uncomfortable.

SIDED WITH THE PANOPTICON?

I attempt to queer my classroom and teaching however I can, through supporting students in their own inquiries. Though I am technically sided with the Panopticon, I politically and methodologically oppose the forces that employ, pay and literally sustain my body and time. I marvel: Has the Panopticon confused me for one of its own? As I have transitioned from being Ms. Krywanczyk to being Mr. Krywanczyk at my school over the past year, this feeling of infiltration has been enhanced. When I was Ms. K, my gender nonnormativity stood out and seemed to beg questions from curious students—why did I look like a boy, what happened to my tits, how long had I known I liked girls? But as Mr. K, the more normatively male I appear over time, the more authority it seems like I have in my classroom and the less my sixth grade students ask about me, personally. For the first time, this year I have felt closeted in my own classroom—both as queer and as trans. The question of "coming out" to my students has been complicated by my experience early on in the year of being a rare model of a (assumed) straight, (assumed) cisgender man who comfortably and proactively discusses LGBTQ affairs. But as the year has progressed, so have my feelings of conflict and guilt.

It is my goal to be visible without self-appointing as an expert or a representative, and without closing discussion about LGBTQ issues in my classroom. But the impact of my transition on my school environment is not ultimately about me, but more about the way certain bodies—mine included—become "seen" and, for better or worse, provoke dialogue. At no point in my transition at my school has my primary concern been for my safety or my feelings. I am an adult with all of the resources I could ever want, including a lifetime of learning how to self-advocate and the protection of employment non-discrimination policy in New York City.

So what does being visible in my school entail for me? It involves stopping by classrooms of 7th and 8th graders who knew me last year as Ms. K to say "hello." It involves advocating for my colleagues to encourage appropriate questions from students, and to embrace the fact that Mr. K is not the only person in the school who can speak to trans issues.

CONCLUSION

In truly queer form, I must say that there is no simple answer to the question of what role my "outness" plays in queering my teaching. My identity and presentation simultaneously do and do not matter in my teaching.

Three weeks ago I made the choice to come out as transgender and as queer to one of my sixth graders. This student has demonstrated a consistent, pointed interest in trans issues and has raised unprovoked questions about transsexuals on at least three occasions. He (or she?) is sometimes teased by other students for "acting gay," wearing sweater-vests, and borrowing pink highlighters from the girls in class to decorate his notebook. Without assuming anything about this student's identity, it is clear that gender and sexuality are important for the student to think about and work through right now. One day, this student approached my desk to ask me about "the difference between 'gender' and 'sex'," citing the transgender woman on the television reality show "The Real World" as evidence that sex and gender are not always the same. I told him that I identify as transgender, and so his observation was very real to me and to many people in my life. I explained that I don't talk much about my history not because I am ashamed of it but because it can be a distraction. The student nodded, surprised to hear that I'm trans but equipped with an implicit understanding of discretion: "I won't tell anyone, Mr. K." The next day, this student placed a Post-it note on my desk with three questions on it: "What did it feel like to change and was it hard?" "Do you feel better now that you know yourself?" and "Do you ever think 'Why did this happen to me'?"

In this particular situation, my "coming out" as a transsexual and as a queer man seemed to be an effectively queer method to provoke questions and challenge assumptions. This anecdote is a salient reminder that there are students of all shapes, sizes, backgrounds, and experiences in every single public school across the nation who could potentially identify in some way with Lawrence King. Queer pedagogy must account for the physical bodies in any classroom and confront the violent specter of the closet without pretending that there are any solid, intact solutions floating around to be spotted and simply grabbed. My "coming out" is not in itself a radical act, nor is it necessarily inherent in a queer pedagogical methodology—but that does not preclude the potential efficacy and significance of acts of "coming out" in public schools, by students and faculty alike. When the act of "coming out" is pushed into further intellectual pursuit rather than presented as a simple and coherent conclusion unto itself, it extends beyond tokenizing LGBT approaches to identity and can even ground queer pedagogy in the material realities and breathing lives it effects.

2

"It Is about Geography and Memory": Coming to Voice with/in/out Academia

Billy Clem

> "In spite of illness, in spite of the arch-enemy sorrow, one can remain alive long past the usual date of disintegration if one is unafraid of change, insatiable in intellectual curiosity, interested in big things, happy in small ways. In the course of sorting and setting down my memories I have learned that these advantages are usually independent of one's merits. . . ."
>
> —Edith Wharton

This is the most difficult writing I have had to do in a long time because this writing is about me. The writing that I need to be doing—a dissertation in literature (going very slowly); comments on yet another student paper (at least 80 waiting); replies and answers to e-mail from students, administrators, or colleagues (innumerable)—is not about me. Furthermore, I have been "trained"—I dislike this word because it makes me feel like a circus dog—not to write about myself because potential literary critics need to distance themselves from the texts about which they write, and I have a difficult time distancing myself from myself. Thus, it can be no wonder that I can hardly accomplish this particular writing, a task that I really need to be doing for me, because it seems, primarily, that I am a full-time community college instructor and a candidate for a PhD in literature; I am, in short, an individual under demanding obligations for my livelihood, and I don't have time for a lot of, if you will, self-indulgence. While working for food, water, shelter, health care that I desperately need because of chronic illnesses (Crohn's disease, arthritis, hypoglycemia), and trying to meet my needs for intellectual discourse and emotional intercourse, I must contend, as a radically feminist disabled gay white man from the lower working class, with dominant and dominating structures of political and personal oppressions in all aspects of my life—personal, political, and professional.

In order to write this narrative, I have had to do two things: first, arrange and rearrange time and work, all of which I am happy to do if not for a publication at least for an attempt to make sense of my thoughts on the intersections of class and sexuality and ability (and all other identity categories) in my life; and second, resist (but acquiesce from "training") the impulse and perhaps requirement to write an academic analysis, for personal writing of this sort, it seems to me, eludes academic conceptualization. Any analysis and/or self-reflection of situation, time, memory, pain, pleasure, and identity require something outside prescription: they require a self-indulgence tempered by a bit of distance and intelligence. Thus, in fashioning a narrative about my growing up in a white, lower working-class family as a gay boy in both Chicago and rural Missouri; about going to college and graduate school and trying to come to voice, or find myself and articulate that self; about understanding what it means to live in a world hostile to any difference from the imperialist, colonialist, white-supremacist and racist, heterosexist, ableist, ageist, biospherically destructive capitalist patriarchy, I must try to write honestly and clearly about my different and differing locations and locutions. So, I'll begin at the beginning, or what I think of as the beginning, and write into the present.

I am the son of two white U.S. (American) citizens both born in the mid-twentieth century to poor and working class families. My mother comes from near total Irish ancestry out of working-class Chicago. Most of the men were cops: her grandfather, father, and many, many uncles and cousins patrolled the streets for years; her father/my grandfather even guarded the first Mayor Daley, a picture of which still hangs in my Mom's home. The women—those very few who received any higher education, an aunt, one sister—were teachers. Perhaps there is a nurse somewhere? The other women were, of course, "homemakers"—an unpaid and often thankless but entirely necessary job. Everybody else in the family got whatever jobs were available, usually "unskilled," meaning undervalued, low-paid labor. This family, the O'Mearas, after decades of struggle, moved out of the Irish-American ghettos into small, all-white working class neighborhoods. Catholics, of course, they eventually assimilated thoroughly and became what people here in the US would call politically conservative; elsewhere, generally fascist, believing in a rather narrow idea of what constitutes humanity—Catholic, white, male, heterosexual, fully abled and aspiring to middle-class respectability. They are a tough-love family, at least, but they maintain ties to one another pretty well; they come together often for christenings, birthday parties, weddings, and funerals. They can put away their beer, and, as South-side Irish, they love the Chicago White Sox, and, of course, da Bears. When I've had the chance to reconnect with this extended family from my mother's side, I find that they are very kind, offering lots of food and their political opinions freely. One can imagine our conversations short and visits infrequent. And the few of us who are a bit different from the standard congregate and smile.

My father's family is mostly Irish, with some Scottish and Cherokee, and there are rumors of African ancestry, though I am the only one willing to discuss or inquire into this aspect. They are very poor, white southerners from rural Tennessee. Bootleggers during prohibition, they can still get you moonshine if you need it. All laborers at one point, a few of the Clems or their familial off-shoots have moved into management positions in what still passes as "blue-collar" labor: construction and/or plumbing. Generous and kind people if you're family, or just exceedingly friendly if you're not, they will feed you all day long. And it's delicious, southern cooking that, for one with Crohn's disease, c'est moi, or any other ailment, can lead rather quickly to a stomach ache that, when reflected upon, was worth the trouble. And the accent is truly lovely. I hardly ever see my father's family because of distance, time, and sadly, on all our parts, interest, but when I hear an east-Tennessee/northern-Georgia accent (think of hearing Loretta Lynn's beautiful voice) I hear my dad and his family immediately. There is something lovely there.

My parents, Catherine and Billy, met in the early 1970s and after just a few months of romance, married against her white, Catholic, middle-class-aspiring family's ideas of appropriate marriage. No doubt, this marrying down, or at least laterally, appealed to her in some way. It appealed to him, too, I think. His non-Catholic upbringing, frank talk, and strange accent undid her family who could not tolerate the idea that one of their own would marry an un(der)educated laborer from the US south. His family was somewhat better about the marriage; his mother already gone, his sisters embraced the beautiful, young, "northern" bride—albeit from a distance of some 500 miles. They made a sort of mixed-marriage, and were, emotionally and financially, on their own.

Their relationship, I believe, was strained at the beginning. A fast marriage, no money, and few prospects for good jobs because he had little high school and she just got through the Chicago public school system of the 1960s with its low standards and racist and sexist problems money was always scarce. Her intolerant family and his far away didn't help. And after becoming pregnant rather quickly, my Mom delivered a baby a year into the marriage who, tragically, died immediately. It seems, from piecing together the story over many years and from hearing my Mom's reflections on this time, that she had little or no support in grieving properly for her lost baby, her first child, and for herself. Her pain is unfathomable to me because it is so profound; I understand it but cannot imagine it thoroughly. My Dad's pain is palpable, though I couldn't swear to it as he and I don't share our feelings and needs as she and I do. Certainly, among US men, sharing feelings isn't always acceptable, and I venture to believe that this is very much the case among poor and working-class men, for shame in capitalism and training in maleness produce feelings of unwanted weakness; though not in all instances, this is certainly the case among many I know. As a result, sometime later, they tried pregnancy again. They decided that if this one took, they'd go on. And so, sometime later, in late 1973, I was born.

With one child now, a coveted boy, their lives seemed to improve. Dad had completed night school to be a truck driver and was now driving for Zenith, and though this job required him to be gone six of seven days each week, it paid well. Mom was now home full-time, no longer working at Burger King where she had been since high school, and enjoyed to some degree staying home with her new baby. It is, I believe, important for me to acknowledge that while she had a child and enjoyed some aspects of motherhood, she missed very much the opportunities that come with working away from home. And though the separations from each other and the worlds they knew were difficult for both of them, more so for her I think as she alone cared full-time for an infant, these were decent days financially. Of course, I have no direct memory of this time, but I imagine them from seeing the pictures and hearing the stories as "fairly good days." A young, good-looking couple, a cute baby with blond hair and blue eyes, and enough money to pay bills and have things make for a decent picture, something American-dream like.

Things began to change when more children came. Though more than happy to have more children, all beautiful and "healthy," the young couple found that money became much tighter with more mouths to feed. Identical twin girls—a surprise at the delivery that more than one baby had come—Catherine and Elizabeth were born in 1975. My Mom became the envy of her family and friends because twins are always something bigger and better. But, with Dad on the road all the time, Mom had no one to help her with three children—a two-year-old and infant twins. Of course, she became depressed and anxious, for who would not under such stress? She found, I believe, little or no sympathy and certainly no help from her family, neighbors, and friends. In fact, recently, my Mom shared with me that, some months after the twins were born, she had asked one of her sisters why she, my Mom, cried all the time and felt terrible. The sister replied that all women felt this way after children were born—and that was the end of the conversation. She had no one to whom she could ask these important questions, no where to go in a time of dire need, no one with whom to cry. And, as one can imagine, the feminist movement had not quite made it to south-side white Irish Chicago and allowed women to seek help from each other. In essence, she sucked it up and did what she could, which, I believe, became a soul-destroying existence. It is little wonder to me now that during my childhood her temper could be short; my Dad's always was, too, after, no doubt, grueling driving and the delivering of TVs. This is, probably, one source of my chronic anxiety: fearing that I'm saying the wrong thing or bothering someone, I have always become nervous when approaching any new situation, even with familiar people.

Two more babies came quickly: Samantha in 1977 and Hollis (Geno) in 1980. Because the money was tight and tighter all the time—this was the late 70s and early 80s with inflation and backlash from anti-civil rights people—Dad was working all the time; with no outside help available, Mom decided the family was big enough. Five little mouths to feed, clothe, and educate was more than plenty—no doubt, it was too much. And though I am very uncomfortable writing this, and though it has taken me years to come to terms with this, I must admit that my parents' drinking became serious. They maintained their jobs, of course, but along with drinking, as anyone growing up around alcoholism can attest, comes abuse and neglect. Though party nights could be fun for us—lots of soda, or pop as it's called in Chicago, and potato chips, late nights of TV, friends sleeping over, and adults sometimes fawning over you—these parties often gave me, as a young boy, a feeling of despondency. I felt lost, afraid, and unsettled. This disorder, or unproductive anarchy, that comes with such drinking parties and loud music, with adults fighting or laughing or loving uncontrollably, with staying up rather late and waking up to hung-over, grumpy parents, made me feel unmoored, made me want stability, order, and permanence. So, as a young boy, I searched without knowing for the people and the place where I would find that stability, order, and permanence I so craved: I found school, and, fortunately for me, therein I flourished.

I loved school as a young boy—absolutely and unconditionally. I loved to read and write, and did so all the time, even when I should have been doing something else. And, in general, I was a good student; eager and bright, I was liked by the teachers and earned good grades. Certainly I had friends with whom I played on the playground during recess, but nothing mattered more than being in the classroom doing schoolwork. I loved worksheets and textbooks and all the good marks I received—all this is good practice indeed for a teacher-to-be. In fact, I loved school so much that I could not bear to be absent. A now-funny story still circulates about my refusing to stay home when sick. In first grade, each student had the opportunity to lead the "Pledge of Allegiance" and conduct some patriotic song by waving his or her right hand in a triangle while standing in front of the class. My turn came the day I was sick with a cold. My parents told me that I could not go to school. I cried and complained, and they sent me back to bed. So, while they sat in the kitchen drinking coffee, I dressed and walked myself to school—as a six-year-old in a large city. This, of course, became something of a capital offense, for walking to school alone was totally forbidden—safety, I'm sure. I can still only imagine the panic they must have felt when they went into my room and did not find me sick in bed, still complaining of the injustice of being made to stay home on what was the most important day of my life thus far! And how they knew to look for me at school makes me laugh aloud today; they knew me well! So, there I was at my desk hearing Mrs. Brown say, "Billy, today is your day to lead us. . ." when I saw my Dad and the school counselor at the classroom door. Immediately, I burst into tears and yelled out how much I wanted to stay at school and lead the class today! Mrs. Brown helped me to gather my stuff and led me to the door. Beyond this, I have no memory of the event, but my parents do and still talk about it: how angry and frightened they were at first and then how perplexed that one of their own was such a nerd so early in life! This illustrates, I think, my early devotion to all things school. This devotion continued even with the devastating move from Chicago to rural southwest Missouri that my family had to make because of my Dad's job's relocation.

This move, coming when I was not quite nine years old, at the end of third grade, was a difficult adjustment for all of us. Rural southwest Missouri is nothing like south-side Chicago, to say the least. The areas share only two characteristics: the same language, in a much different accent and an unbounded whiteness. The move devastated my Mother who was moving from all she knew and loved: her parents, friends, and the great city of Chicago. She had lived in this community her entire life and thought of herself as a member of a working-class culture that, whatever its problems, was comfortable in many ways: neighbors could sometimes be depended upon in an emergency, and the sharing of some material resources was a given; these hallmarks of working-class communities did not/do not exist in this new place in Misery, what we came to call our new state. Leaving all this for a small town in Missouri would be/was miserable for her. But my Father was fine with it. He had moved often and traveled constantly, so this wouldn't be too much of a change; furthermore, he'd be moving back to the south—albeit a different region but still the south. And it seems that he had won the silent contest with his father-in-law: my mother and these kids would be entirely dependent upon him, my Father, alone. And he was now a landowner. My siblings, so small and under six years old, seemed fine with it. I hated the idea of this move and its completion. I remember vividly my Mom's coming into my bedroom to tell me that we were going to live in Marshfield, Missouri. I couldn't believe it and begged her not to make us go; all I could picture was the scenery in Little House on the Prairie: a badly-leaning home and a one-room schoolhouse with bitchy Nellie Olsen ordering us all around! Of course, Marshfield and its school were not exactly the world of Laura Ingalls Wilder, mercifully, but it was, and still is, a place about which I am at best ambivalent because of its right-wing, fundamentalist Christian ideology and its open, hostile racism, sexism, classism, heterosexism, ableism, and ageism. But the landscape, the Ozark Mountains and valleys, the old winding roads, the communities of Amish peoples, is incomparable. And some of its nearly all-white-population were/could be kind and caring—especially the teachers, which is no surprise. It is, at least, an interesting place, one full of contradictions for someone like me.

Their funny accents, their not taking to me because I was not like anything they knew, and my isolation were both a source of pain and wonder to me from as early as fourth grade. It was clear immediately that my family was not middle-class in a town that valued conservative, white, Protestant values of obedience to a vengeful, Old Testament God, immaculate lawns, small families, and the pretensions of upward mobility through capitalist connections. This petite-bourgeois was quite content with its sterility and unquestioned hostility to outsiders. And we were loud, strange, and poor. We had a nice house at the edge of town, purchased and financed with inheritance money from one of my Mom's "maiden" aunts—a home that has been foreclosed upon, now as I write, by a bank after twenty-five years of payments due to what we hear in the news media is a "recent mortgage crisis"—but my parents drank beer and smoked cigarettes outside by our pool, and we ran around, as one of my classmates' mother's said to him, as "unsupervised" children. This remark continues to be a source of much amusement. My truck-driver father cursed often and made fun of other people openly. My Mom was constantly asked if she knew Al Capone. And money issues abounded; there was never enough for everything, and the constant worry over paying the bills, losing or not losing the house, having another car repossessed, was ever present. And while my siblings seemed to be fine, most of the kids who pronounced the word "the" as "thee" said I ran like a girl and that I was funny looking because my dark eyebrows didn't match my blond hair. Over time, I found that I had neither aptitude for nor interest in the things that most but not all of the other boys valued: sports, hunting, money, and objectifying and harassing (hating but wanting to possess) girls. Moving from elementary school through junior high school, puberty, on into high school, and realizing that I had feelings and ideas not universally shared but openly denigrated—finding sports boring, guns frightening, money pointless if not divisive, and girls to be equals and friends and boys to be those for whom I had sexual feelings—forced me to try to make myself invulnerable to a hostile world, to build an invisible wall that no one could penetrate. Frighteningly, I thought this worked for a long time. Realizing that what I heard at school, in the culture, and at home about myself and other people—that African Americans were criminals, Asians evil geniuses, gays sick and wrong, the disabled an unwanted and unnecessary burden, the poor destitute because of laziness, women stupid and pliant—contradicted everything I knew, felt, and believed. It contradicted my entire existence, and I could not countenance it: it made no sense to me ever to be self-hating and/or to hate others who had never wronged me. Naturally I have always been disposed to like people, to get along if not with genuine affection at least with civility. But I was forced, because I could not and would not participate, financially or emotionally, in the activities that others participated in, into near-total isolation and impenetrability. I shared my feelings with no one.

Mercifully, the other part of school, the part that I had always loved, was still present: learning, reading, writing, and teachers. While my social and familial worlds were sometimes very difficult, this other world, one in which I thrived, was still available to me. I had teachers, those in English and History of course, who loved, favored, and nurtured me. Though I was a terrible music student who was always last-chair trombone, I loved music deeply and wanted very much to be good at it, to do justice at least to its beauty and power. It turned out later that I had a decent tenor voice and could carry a tune. I enjoyed student clubs and organizing and leading activities that brought about learning, which tells you how much of a dork I am. I loved learning rudimentary French and Spanish and reading history books, Shakespeare, long novels, and poetry. (And secretly, and I've never told this to anyone, I longed to run track but could not because of lack of strength and asthma; this interests me now for what it means for that time: running: running for/from what?) In this respect, school was wonderful—until something nearly calamitous occurred: I read books that negated my existence.

In high school, I was wounded by two books and a teacher's reading of one of these books that I was required to read for classes. Of course, there were many other wounds, inflicted by students and teachers alike—name calling and/or general pronouncements on groups of people—but in reading and learning, which I had loved so much, which was not an escape but a clarification, the pain was much harder to endure. The wall I had built was more permeable than I had imagined. First, as a junior in English class, while reading The Great Gatsby, a teacher whom I loved and whom I know loved me, made a point of condemning F. Scott Fitzgerald's anti-Semitism while praising his heterosexism and homophobia in this important, well-written, early twentieth-century US novel. She pointed out that Mr. McKee, "a pale feminine man from the flat below" (34) was obviously a homosexual whose inability to shave properly marks him as different from the others. She went on to laugh about how homosexuals always work hard on their appearance only to fail at it eventually. A message about (compulsory) heterosexuality if ever there is one. Of course, the text validates this when Gatsby says, "Taking out my handkerchief, I wiped from his cheek the remains of spot of dried lather that had worried me all afternoon" (41). I turned red, certainly, at the mere mention of this idea and was pained by her hateful mocking. I do not remember even recalling this character or these events during my initial reading, but upon discussion and later readings I was chagrined, at least, believing that she was talking directly to me. Absurd, I know; real, nonetheless. How could I, a boy just recently shaving his own face, trying hard after shaving to clean up before school, not be wounded by this? And to this day still I think of that character and that classroom conversation as I clean up from shaving. I wonder if these kinds of messages ever go away or clear themselves up, if pain ever dissolves, or if it can be transformed. Ultimately, I think yes but only after much distress and work.

The next year, my senior year, I would encounter this again, not directly in class discussion but simply during my own reading. While reading Emily Brontë's Wuthering Heights and being repulsed by the ubiquitous violence but interested in the class-critique and ill-fated matches, I was taken aback by the narrator and his hateful description of Linton Heathcliff as the sickly and feminine son who is party to evil. After the interpretation of The Great Gatsby, how could I not, again, find the character I identified as gay—right or wrong—both to be me and not be me? How could I not be hurt again by reading and interpretation if every gay person in a book is somehow wrong or evil? My love for language and narrative, for the entire concept of reading, was challenged: if that which had been so interrogative and soothing turned back on me, as so much else had, the question became not how could I go on loving it but what can I do now?

So, I did what I had to do: I kept my mouth shut, and I went to college.

Of course, there had been no question that I would go to college after an above average high school academic career: the question was how and where I would go to college. My family had no money for college applications and certainly no money for tuition, room and board, and/or books; with five children living on a small salary in rural southwest Missouri, money was so scarce that paying for one kid's college was out of the question. Furthermore, none of us could understand why a college would even charge a fee to apply. My parents said, "Don't you have to pay when you get there? There are better, more important things to do with money." I had just assumed, naively, that education was free. With these constraints, I applied to the one college without an application fee that I could find. Culver-Stockton College, in northeast Missouri on the western bank of the Mississippi River, happened to be a private liberal arts school where I might indulge myself in reading great books, in being required to read great books, and a place where I might have a chance to make the beginnings of a new life.

No, this will not become the typical narrative in which the son goes to college on both scholarships and many loans, of course, attains education, lives a bourgeois life, and, as a consequence, sees his first homelife differently and then rejects it. I had already seen it differently: I knew that something, many things, were very wrong. I knew that a controlling and abusive father, a man frustrated by lack of money, privilege, and power because of his societal status, was wrong. I knew that a controlled and beleaguered mother, someone trying to have some pleasure in life but unable to find it, was wrong. I knew that the direction in which my siblings were headed, the direction they have often followed—drug addiction, arrests, abuse, unemployment—was all wrong. (I am happy to write that some of my siblings are now clean and doing very well, trying to build a new life though many obstacles remain). I knew that the desire both to be somewhere else and with them was impossible to actualize and painful to comprehend. I knew that the small town in which we lived, a place that cannot be called a community, was wrong for its laughable classism and virulent racism, heterosexism, sexism, that believing poor people, people of color, gays and lesbians, the disabled, and women were less-than-human was wrong. I knew that the school system in which I had received most of my primary education was like most other institutions: merely a microcosm of the idiocy of the larger world, complete with its bigotry-in-power and its moribund ideas. But I did not possess or even have access to the language that would help me to understand, both emotionally and intellectually, what all this meant and what the future could be. And at this time, when I was 17 and leaving for college, I had no doubt that a good future was available to me; now, with the world in the state it is in, in the state it has always been, I worry about a future for any being. It would be sometime, more than a year after finishing the BA, before I could read and apply to my own life these words from Toni Morrison's Nobel Lecture in Literature: "Oppressive language does more than represent violence; it is violence; it does more than represent the limits of knowledge; it limits knowledge. . . . Sexist language, racist language, theistic language, all are typical of the policing languages of mastery and cannot, do not permit new knowledge or encourage the mutual exchange of ideas" (14). Leaving home and going into higher education led me to find texts, like Morrison's, that allowed me to put words with ideas and feelings; going to college and graduate school enabled me to turn chaos and disorder into some kind of coherent meaning.

An example, perhaps my most salient one, comes from when I found and read, on my own, Audre Lorde's poetry. Reading her words, understanding her meanings, listening to her clear, strong voice on the page enabled me to put together the disparate thoughts swirling in my brain, those thoughts that kept me awake at night wondering what anything meant. There I was, a gay white guy from the working class, working on a Master's degree in English at Southwest Missouri State University (now Missouri State University), unable to use language—to talk with or to anyone—to free myself from the constraints placed on me by bigotry and misunderstanding and, finally, to begin talking with others. Lorde's poem, "Echoes," opened up language and the world to me:

> There is a timbre of voice
> that comes from not being heard
> and knowing you are not being
> heard noticed only
> by others not heard
> for the same reason. (7)

Although Emily Dickinson says, "If I feel physically as if the top of my head were taken off, I know that is poetry," I must say that when my head is put back on, I know I've read poetry. Now, through Lorde's poem, I had a language in which to talk and to recontextualize everything about myself, everything I knew: that racism, ethnocentrism, classism, caste systems, sexism, gender hierarchy, heterosexism, ableism, ageism, regionalism, nationalism, speciesism, and environmental destruction were and are the problems coming from capitalism and patriarchy—and, importantly, that I both benefited from and lost myself in these machinations. I had been right: I was not wrong, and I had a voice that I could, must use to make things that are wrong right. I went on to find Lorde's essays in Sister Outsider and learned to understand and say that the "master's tools will never dismantle the master's house" and that

> [t]hose of us who stand outside the circle of this society's definition of acceptable women [and being]; those of use who have been forged in the crucibles of difference—those of use who are poor, who are lesbians, who are Black, who are older [who are other]—know that survival is not an academic skill. It is learning how to stand alone, unpopular and sometimes reviled, and how to make common cause with those others identified as outside the structures in order to define and seek a world in which we can all flourish. (112)

Clearly, Lorde's language, coming from and foundational for the thoughts of Black Lesbian Feminism, helped me to see and hear everything anew; Lorde reached across time and space, through print and voice, and helped a young, chronically ill, gay white boy from the lower working class to become a radically feminist being doing the work that he needs to do, living a life that he needs to live. Her words continue to help me to read and reread; they help me to relive and flourish.

It was and has been learning in and outside higher education, both undergraduate and graduate schools, that has given me the language to articulate a more complete, complex understanding of my personal and political relations to myself and to the rest of the world. This has been my liberation, my being set free from the multiple oppressions of classism, heterosexism, racism, sexism, ableism, ageism, and biospheric destruction. Going to college, but more specifically graduate school at Southwest Missouri State University and Northern Illinois University and reading black and lesbian feminist poets, novelists, and essayists and understanding the radical potential in Shakespeare's outsider-bastards, Aaron, Jacques, Edmond, has enabled me to confirm that I had not been wrong, that I am not wrong: that my being is more than okay; my being is acceptable and necessary. I didn't exactly need a boost to my self-esteem; I simply needed some questions to be answered, some confirmation. Finding these literary and cultural texts and a few supportive, good friends has allowed me to answer my urgent, unformed questions and to find ways to tear down that wall of false invulnerability, to connect with others, and to begin to attempt to flourish as a being in the world.

I must admit, uncomfortably so, that I never questioned the idea that education belonged to me, that reading and learning were mine to be indulged and enjoyed, and that I would someday be a teacher or professor and do something good in the world. I was a good student in high school, and my teachers encouraged, helped, and indulged me. In higher education, I have/found professors to do the same. This has led me to believe that neither am I a stranger in paradise nor have I landed in this fine place so far from home,[1] for the academy is neither paradisiacal nor fine, even if it is a better space than other spaces. I have to remind people all the time the better does not mean good: better simply means not as bad as something before or something else, which implies that the fully right is still to be achieved. While institutions of higher education are troubled and beset with multiple oppressions emanating from law makers' positions, tax payers' desires, administrators' restraints, and some professors' and students' beliefs, the actual task, joy, and love of learning have been available to me; they should be available to everyone.

Of course, I am now able to understand more clearly, after years of reading and writing and collaborating with others, what it means that all this has been open to me; this means that white boys who meet some of the arbitrary standards can be given a pass, can have an entrance into the life of the mind or access to a decent paycheck. But, to be honest, the issue is more complicated. In order to survive throughout much of my life, I have had to be silent about social class, sexuality, race, ethnicity, gender, age, ability, and the environment—at times while in college and graduate school and certainly in my current job at a conservative community college on the edges of suburban and rural Illinois. I could not/have not been allowed to interrogate or protest openly what I saw/see to be wrong—the ridicule of lower class peoples; the open hostility and bigotry directed at sexual others;

the obvious exclusion and stereotyping of people of color; the derogatory "jokes" made at women's expense; the refusal to acknowledge dis/abled people and people outside a particular age-range as fully human and valuable; the barefaced disregard for and abuse of other animals and ecosystems—without ramification. I could not acknowledge my own pain and/or privileges, and I have had plenty of both. With the language I learned on my own from the springboard of the academy and in collaboration with professors and other students and a few friends, I can articulate a position that validates my claims that I am no stranger in a fine paradise and that I and all other beings and non-beings laboring and choking under oppressions of any kind must take what we can from education and community and use this to create a new, radically different world. I now understand that growing up as an/other in US cultures was a benefit—not a liability. I understand more clearly that growing up poor and working class and being chronically ill, that being surrounded by people who are not deceitful or pretentious but genuinely helpful and caring, gives me the ability to be the same: to be myself, to be honest, and to love the earth and its inhabitants. And growing up gay, I think, enabled me to understand what compounded outsider status really is: that to be alone and ridiculed is painful and that to acknowledge pain is crucial for healing and living and, eventually, flourishing. I suppose being gay, disabled, and working class has allowed me to feel sympathy and empathy not only for other people but for other creatures and things as well; this location, these pieces of my identity, have enabled me to connect, help, and flourish.

Writing this narrative, and reflecting back on painful and pleasurable episodes in my life has been a most difficult task. Reliving so many memories and choosing and editing what to share (and what not to share) in order to attempt to make clear my meaning but not to violate myself or others could be at times overwhelming and disconcerting. No doubt, this narrative seems disorganized, or at least, disjunctive, perhaps foreshortened, even pointless. But isn't that the way memory and geography exist? Isn't this how we come to meaning, even if that meaning is unstable and temporary? Meanings are fragmented, patchy, often disconnected; our task as humans with consciousness, I think, is to attempt to connect, to build bridges to one another across time, space, politics, true or false consciousness, location, and locution, and then come together for what is good and right. I cannot say with honesty that I could understand or believe this if I had different origins or different educational and reading experiences.

Just the other day, I finished reading Zadie Smith's novel, *On Beauty*. It is an excellent novel by a young, brilliant writer, but it is more than just good writing, more than novelistic virtuosity. Its meaning is profound, I think. Structured loosely on and going beyond E.M. Forster's novel Howard's End, Smith's *On Beauty* interrogates humans' relations with ourselves, others, and the worlds in which we live in a way that few novels can or do. The novel brings together people of seemingly dissimilar backgrounds, from different places, with different ideas, and forces them to communicate, perhaps even to resolve, their differences. In short, two of the characters, Kiki Belsey and Carlene Kipps, women of the African diaspora, wives of academic men on opposite sides of all issues, men who dominate all they participate in, including their marriages, come together and learn from each other that to hear one another, to be open and vulnerable, that to share and to love, is to flourish. I will not give away the novel's ending or meaning (you should just read it), but I will tell you this: at the last moment, when virtually all is lost, the reader finds out that one of the women has written the other a note with the words that tear down the unnecessary walls we build, the words that help us into being a radically new world: "There is such a shelter in each other." Indeed.

NOTE

1. Titles from two early texts about academics from the working class: Strangers in Paradise: Academics from the Working Class. Ed. Jack Ryan and Charles Sackrey. Boston: South End Press, 1984; & This Fine Place so far from Home: Voices from Academics from the Working Class. Ed. C.L. Barney Dews and Carolyn Leste Law. Philadelphia: Temple University Press, 1995. The former takes its title from a popular song, "Stranger in Paradise," from the musical Kismet, recorded by Tony Bennett in 1953.

BIBLIOGRAPHY

Brontë, Emily. Wuthering Heights. New York: Penguin, 1996.
Fitzgerald, F. Scott. The Great Gatsby. New York: Simon & Schuster, 1995.
Forster, E.M. *Howards End*. New York: Penguin, 2000.
Lorde, Audre. "Echoes." The Marvelous Arithmetics of Distance. New York: Norton, 1993.
——. "The Master's Tools Will Never Dismantle the Master's House." Sister Outsider: Essays and Speeches by Audre Lorde. Freedom, CA: Crossing, 1984.
Morrison, Toni. The Nobel Lecture in Literature, 1993. New York: Knopf, 1996.
Smith, Zadie. On Beauty. New York: Penguin, 2005.
Wharton, Edith. A Backward Glance. New York: Simon & Schuster, 1998.

3

Rhetorics of Disgust and Indeterminacy in Transphobic Acts of Violence[1]

Em McAvan

Last year in Greeley, Colorado, a young Latina transsexual woman named Angie Zapata was brutally murdered. Her murderer Allen Andrade is reported to have said to police that he killed "it," and that "gay things need to die."[2] Yet Angie Zapata appears to have seen herself not as a gay man, but as a heterosexual woman. In the news stories about the case, her family refer to her by the appropriate female pronouns and talk about a gender presentation and desire to go on hormones in ways that are unambiguously *transsexual*, rather than homosexual. Andrade's chilling statement that "gay things need to die," then, is not just simple misrecognition (though it is that), but rather a revealing comment about the ways in which transphobic violence remains entangled in a gender-related homophobia. That is, violence against transsexuals remains explicitly tied to gender variance, such that transsexual and transgendered people's identifications are simultaneously negated (Angie Zapata as "really a man") *and* placed outside of a male/female binary. Although Andrade was eventually convicted of first-degree murder as a hate crime,[3] the assumptions behind both her murder and the news coverage of the murder and trial remain largely unquestioned within the society tasked with bringing her murderer to justice.

What I want to do in this paper, then, is reflect upon the ways in which media reports of violence perpetuated against transsexual, transgender and gender non-conforming people (most especially trans women of color) place the victims into a zone of indeterminacy.[4] Rather than a clear categorization as "trans," "male," "female," "gay," "straight," "cross-dresser," and so on, I argue that all of these markers and more are mobilized into a public performance of disgust that rather than cancel each other out, instead pile upon each other to position the gender-variant victims of violence as decidedly *not* human. As we shall see when I discuss the coverage of Sanesha Stewart's murder in New York in 2007, blatant contradictions continue to operate in media coverage of transphobic violence. Just as the trans body is made to slide between transsexual and gay, when reports offer pre-emptive versions of the notorious "trans panic" defense, so does the reporting slide from journalist's point-of-view to that of the killer. Moreover, such an overdetermined state of the trans body is profoundly influenced by other discourses about gender and the monstrous, from sensationalist talk shows to serial killer slasher movies.

TRANS REPRESENTATION IN NEWS MEDIA

Transsexual and transgendered people have long been a figure of fascination and disgust in our culture, typically being analysed as pathological in medical and psychological discourse, or in sensationalist fashion in the media. And if stories about murdered trans people can be redoubled in perversity with salacious sex or prostitution angles, then so much the better.[5] Coupled with the sensationalism is a persistently use of what Julia Serano calls cissexism—"the belief that transsexuals' identified genders are inferior to, or less authentic than, those of *cissexuals* (i.e., people who are not transsexual)" (12).[6]

Serano argues media depictions of trans women (who are the overwhelming majority of murdered trans people), are depicted through a number of formalized, repetitious tropes. She argues that media depictions bifurcate between two particular tropes—"the deceptive transsexual" and "the pathetic transsexual" (36). Whilst the "pathetic" trans woman will never be read as female (and is thus less of a threat), the deceiver features in the notorious "trans panic" defense—she passes seamlessly as a cissexual woman, duping the men she dates into thinking she is a "real" woman until the inevitable discovery of her genitals. As Talia Mae Bettcher argues, "fundamental to transphobic representations of trans [. . .] people as deceivers is an appearance-reality contrast between gender presentation and sexed body" (48). These transphobic representations ground themselves in un-remarked upon violations of trans bodies—in the repetition of his confession, Andrade admits to grasping at Zapata's genitals, a sexual assault which becomes elided and instead presented as a verification of the "truth" of Angie Zapata's sexed body.[7]

The deceiver is the predominant mode of media description for Angie Zapata, since news stories clearly establish an appearance-reality contrast between her presentation and "biological" sexed body. The "reality" of the sexed body is achieved through the persistently ungendering of trans people's identifications, since despite the official APA guidelines on covering transgendered people, reporters frequently make a number of key mistakes. These include using the term "transvestite" to describe transsexual or transgendered women,[8] using the wrong pronouns (for instance, see Hayes and Lemire), referring to the person as "really" or "actually" male or female (whichever sex they were assigned at birth) and mentioning the trans person's former name regardless of relevance. All of these add up to a consistent construction of trans people's gender identities as fake, illusory, and deceptive.

Consider the following story in *The Denver Post*: "Alan Andrade told his girlfriend that he 'snapped' when he learned the woman he had oral sex with the night before was biologically a man. Indeed, until he confronted eighteen-year-old Angie Zapata in her Greeley apartment in July, Andrade had no reason to believe she was born Justin Zapata" (Whaley "Transgender Girl's"). Dunn in *The Greeley Tribune*, too, repeats that Angie Zapata was "biologically a man named Justin Zapata" ("Smile"), as does Peters. So, the slippage comes from "biologically a man" (an already dubious proposition, given the proliferation and incompleteness of scientific research on the causes of transsexualism, not to mention the fact that a good number of trans people experience their pre-transition lives as always-already their chosen gender) to naming Angie as Justin. The repetition of the assigned name conflates it with a biological maleness, seeming to suggest, I think, that this has somehow been hidden in part by Angie's name. That we are working on the grounds of ontology seems clear, since the "actually" begins from a cissexual primal origin birth moment that cannot be changed but only concealed—Angie is "biologically" once-and-forever Justin. Of course, this is nonsensical, for how is someone *born* a name, and why is that relevant nineteen years later? The citation of the originary birth moment ("it's a boy!"), as Susan Stryker points out, "seizes upon specific material qualities of the flesh, particularly the genitals, as outward indication of future reproductive potential" ("Smile") and continues to function as a sign that forever fixes the trans subject under the sign of cissexual "biology." While names are of course changeable over time, in this mythical gender economy, the self-definitions of trans people become subordinated to the circulation of cissexual ontological propositions as "truth."

So when the *Greeley Tribune* reports that Zapata was "actually a man" (Dunn, "Andrade's Murder Confession") it at once marks a continuity of cissexual assumption between the general public and the transphobic killer, a negation of the trans person's identification that clears the ground for the notorious "trans panic" legal defence (namely, that a person was so surprised by their lover being trans that they were simply *forced* to kill them in an act of panic). The public formed by such an articulation is an implicitly cissexual one, one that identifies (and sympathises) with the cissexual killer rather than the transsexual victim. Indeed, (mis) gendering Angie as male was a core strategy of Andrade's defence case, where his lawyers referred to Angie *only* as "Justin" and "he" (Dunn, "Angie Zapata's friends").

This becomes clearer when we examine another case, this time in New York. The murder of Sanesha Stewart in 2007 by a man she had been seeing for several months was covered by the *New York Daily News* who, without any solid evidence on either score, initially used the headline "Fooled John Stabbed Bronx Tranny" (Hayes and Lemire 2008).[9] The assumption that Stewart, because she was a trans woman of color, was automatically a sex worker plays into stereotypes of trans women as oversexualized, and those of women of color as sexually available—indeed, it is clear that this is a specifically racialized form of transphobia *and* what Serano calls trans-misogyny (15). Both "tranny" and "hooker" here (which appears in the revised story title) signify Stewart's disposability. She is clearly *not* a person a public should mourn for. Further, deception on the part of the murdered trans woman is automatically assumed, despite the fact that it later came out that the alleged killer had known Stewart for months (Moore). The "trans panic" story, then, becomes cynically deployed by a killer, knowing that it "makes sense" to a cissexual public, which then becomes uncritically passed on, with added insults, by a tabloid newspaper.

But rather than neatly fitting into a "deceptive trans woman" trope, I want to show how the coverage vacillates between deceptive and pathetic, passable and unpassable. The article states (wrongly) that the suspect was "the prostitute's john who became enraged when he learned his partner was not a woman" (Hayes and Lemire). And yet, "'she looked like a girl but when she turned around, you knew it was a man' a seventeen-year-old neighbor said. 'She had a big jaw and an Adam's apple'" (Hayes and Lemire). Stewart, it seems, was somehow both deceptive to her lover *and* easily readable as trans to the general public. That this is an obvious contradiction seems irrelevant to the coverage (and presumably to the predominantly cissexual readership).

Thus we can see how the institutional and the social—institutions are after all staffed by people (who read newspapers, who hear politicians or religious leaders like the Pope denounce trans people, etc.)—work as a feedback loop to produce the trans body as aberrant, something to be protected from rather than something in need of institutional protection or defence. Paradoxically, it is murdered trans people who are positioned as criminals, always-already deceptive in misaligning gender presentation and sexed body, or the mere act of changing name. That the trans body is supposed to be read as a threat is explicitly signalled by Allen Andrade's attorney, who called Angie Zapata's smile a "highly provoking act" (Whaley, "Smile").

LOCATING THE UNLOCATABLE

It seems necessary to stress that there is a rather large gulf between the indeterminacy accorded trans subjects by the normative presumptions of cissexist culture and the self-identifications of trans people. Whilst a trans woman may identify as simply female, and this needs to be respected, the effects of such an identification are nevertheless profoundly *not* simple when one considers the discursive and medical regimes mobilized in and after the fact of an instance of transphobic violence. Instead, I find it productive to trace the ways in which trans people are rendered as culturally indeterminate, regardless of identification, gender presentation, hormone and surgical status, since, as Talia Mae Bettcher has pointed out, even "the status of a post-surgical trans [. . .] person is both controvertible and fragile" (49). And indeed, to follow Jay Prosser's suggestion, it remains an essential task of any trans theory to "highlight the costs to the subject of not being locatable in relation to sexual difference" (204).

What is important to note is that indeterminacy is not a product of trans bodies themselves. As Paisley Currah astutely notes, trans "bodies [. . .] have unexpected configurations in their particular *geographies*—for example, breasts with penises for some, male chests with vaginas in others—that produce a dissonance [which] belongs not to the trans body but to those gazers who have conventional gender expectations" (331). So whilst a particular trans geography, like that of a trans woman with a penis, may be absolutely locatable in relation to sexual difference with regards to identification and gender presentation (for instance, Angie Zapata is reported to have said "I'm all woman"), the particular geography of that body is *nevertheless* located by a cissexual gaze as outside, in-between, or indeterminate. What is foreclosed from that then is a trans experience that may or may not assign dissonance to the body topography—most notably, those trans people who do not desire surgery or those for whom genitality (more often likely to be a cissexual concern) may be irrelevant and not connect with gender presentation.[10] To spell that out more clearly, the notion that genitals always define who is "actually" a man, that they "verify" the reality of the sexed body, is wrong and indeed profoundly harmful for many trans subjects. The unveiling of the sexed body, then, does not reveal the "truth," rather it reveals the cissexual assumptions that necessarily equate genitalia with sex and gender and negate trans identifications because of it.

So what seems apparent from the articulation of Angie Zapata as an it, a thing, is that normative gendering appears to condition the very grounds of possibility of what is considered human. How "the human" is mobilized—always against its opposite "the monster," a position that trans people come to occupy through their abjection by rhetorical signifiers of disgust—is precisely the central question of this chapter. This restricted and restrictive conceptualization of "the human" is produced against an on-going violence against transsexual, transgendered and gender-normative communities that is legitimated by social, media and legal discourses alike.

Indeed, through this "itness," the re-writing of trans bodies as indeterminate, against and above self-identification, in itself constitutes a form of violence to trans subjectivity. Yet this rhetorical move occupies a strange temporality—preceding the act of violence and then legitimising it after the fact. Arguably, Angie Zapata's overdetermined production as indeterminate, in the context of a sexual relationship, contributed towards her murder. It is not merely, I think, that killers of trans women hate their victims for their transness. Rather, the acts themselves are over-determined. First, there is the obvious fact that both Zapata and Stewart were women of color, which given the lack of value accorded women of color in a racist society and their construction as threat, must be accounted for. Further, it is arguable that it is the co-mingling of desire (many murders occur amongst sexual partners) and disgust, not to mention the contagion of homosexuality that proves unbearable. The method of the murder itself suggests a degree of violence akin to needing to purge Zapata from the world—Andrade punched her, knocking her to the ground, then hit her with a fire extinguisher, then later when she began to come to, hit her again until she was dead (Dunn, "Andrade's Murder Confession"). Indeed, this confession-that-doesn't-confess places the presumed cissexual and heterosexual audience into the time of the transphobic act itself. By positioning Zapata as a sub-human thing, it evades the question of culpability, for it hasn't been a *real* person who has been murdered. Instead, ventriloquised by the media, Andrade is made to appeal to a cissexual common-sense, asking what heterosexual man, deceived and forced into homosexuality against his will, *wouldn't* do such a thing?[11]

MAKING (TRANS) MONSTERS

The contradictions inherent in the news coverage of murdered trans women can be analysed by a look at the *literariness* of what is ostensibly "realistic" coverage. Literary critic Edward J. Ingebretson has argued compellingly in *At Stake* that the apparently non-fictional news genres have become thoroughly Gothic. As such, these genres require monsters—phallic mothers, murderous black men, gender-ambiguous serial killers, and so on. Ingebretson's work argues fairly conclusively that the presentation of "real life" news is largely a matter of Gothic monstrosity—"real-life" killers are framed through the narrative conventions of fictional texts. What I want to suggest though, is that in cases featuring murdered transsexual and transgendered women, it is instead the *victims* who are framed as monstrous. Indeed, the Gothic news, together with talk shows and horror movies work to police the boundaries of gender, sexuality, race and class. They produce monstrous bodies to be repulsed by, and in doing so constitute the presumed normatively gendered viewing subject.

Yet while these signs of monstrosity coalescence around a "real" person, it is arguable that trans bodies are fictionalised through the media, made monstrous themselves. Jeffrey Jerome Cohen in his introduction to *Monster Theory* suggests that "the monster's body is a cultural body [. . .] a construct and a projection, the body exists only to be read" (4). Etymologically, the term itself comes from the Latin *monstrum*, meaning "that which reveals" (4). The monster, then, does not of itself have its own life or agency, but exists only for its audience. But if it seems on the one hand denied independent existence, it is the emotions of its audience that animate it, for "the monster's body quite literally incorporates fear, desire, anxiety and fantasy (ataractic or incendiary), giving them an independence existence of their own" (4).

Indeed, this notion that bodies are projections of fear and anxiety may account for the contradictions in the coverage of Sanesha Stewart's murder and the affective rhetoric that place Angie Zapata as an "it," "actually a man," *and* female. Written through this lens of the monstrous, the blatant incoherence of the textual construction of Sanesha Stewart's body in the *New York Daily News* seems clear—a projection of cissexual anxieties and prejudices about trans bodies that demands both that trans difference be readable *and* that trans deception be mobilized to suture the anxieties about normative cissexuality and heterosexuality opened up by a sexually active heterosexual trans woman. Whilst this is a task impossible for a material, embodied woman, to be simultaneously readable and unreadable, cast in newsprint the task is more easily achieved. Similarly, the overdetermination of Angie Zapata as an attractive young woman, "biologically Justin Zapata," "it" and a "gay thing" cannot *but* be seen as a projection of cissexual and heterosexual anxiety.

So a monstrous construction of trans bodies creates a vertiginous slide between signifiers—gender, sexuality, race, class, human, non-human. The construction of transgendered bodies as culturally monstrous is in dialogue with other monstrosities with which they have no necessary or even logical connection—homosexuality, "cross" dressing, child abuse—since as we know, most child abusers are straight men, as are those who cross dress for sexual pleasure, and while there are of course gay trans people this is hardly a certainty. Because monsters have to be everything the human is not, this ambiguity is important; they are in the broadest sense *queer*, and comes to take on cultural anxieties about gender, sexuality, race, class, and so on. Whilst obviously, many of these are not strictly transsexual or transgendered; they are nevertheless relevant because, as Andrade's comments confirm, our heterosexist society so frequently conflates trans genders with queer sexualities. Indeed, as Andrew Sharpe has argued, this is even a presumption that guides lawmakers, for example, "in marriage law we will see that, irrespective of sex reassignment surgery, the transgender body is presented as bearing a much more proximate relation to homosexuality" (90). And so it becomes clear that the incoherent, moving indeterminacy of signifiers attached to Angie Zapata and Sanesha Stewart's bodies illustrates the way in which transgendered bodies are constructed as culturally monstrous and the symbolic, the discursive, works to overdetermine the material.

Unsurprisingly then, the monstrous has been a trope of transgender studies since at least Susan Stryker's "My Words to Victor Frankenstein Above the Village of Chamonoix" paper, in which she claims a place for herself as a monster and refuses a humanist ontology of the gendered body for its hidden heterosexist and transphobic positions. She says that, "words like 'creature,' 'monster,' and 'unnatural' need to be reclaimed by the transgendered. By embracing and accepting them, even piling them on top of another, we may dispel their ability to harm us." But while Stryker's words remain a powerful piece of rhetoric, and I'm sure that claiming a monstrous identity is empowering, I remain ambivalent as to the effectiveness of claiming monstrosity, since excessive parody of stereotypes can have the unfortunate side-effect of merely adding fuel to the fire. And more generally, categories of the monstrous perform a normalising cultural function; working to secure the normative against its transgression, usually through a normative, often violent, closure. This last is most crucial when considering the ways in which the monstrous bodies of trans women are positioned within news discourse. While for Cohen, "the monster always escapes" (4), Angie Zapata and Sanesha Stewart were not so lucky.

FEAR AND DISGUST IN GREELEY

Feminist scholars like Julia Kristeva and Sara Ahmed have sought to show how feelings like horror, disgust and shame are discursively formed; related to the power relations of race, class, gender, sexuality and disability with which much contemporary humanities research addresses itself to. In other words, feelings are not culturally neutral; rather they are always-already mediated through cultural sedimentations and citations, performative in the sense that Judith Butler has used it. William Ian Miller, too, argues that disgust "is a moral and social sentiment [and] plays a motivating and confirming role in moral judgement [. . .] It ranks people and things in a kind of cosmic ordering" (2). So what does it mean to express disgust at a trans person's transness?

Sara Ahmed argues in her compelling *The Cultural Politics of Emotion* that disgust works to organise power relations between "above and below, through which 'aboveness' and 'belowness' become properties of particular bodies, objects and spaces (89)." Such affective reactions to a transgendered body works to organise gender normative (usually heterosexual) bodies above, and trans below. As Ahmed is careful to point out, it is not that "belowness" is a state of ontological being, rather that the disgusted reaction works to produce both normative and aberrant bodies at the same time. Categories of fear and disgust are mobilised "to align bodily and social space [. . .], to enable some bodies to inhabit and move in public space through restricting the mobility of other bodies to spaces that are enclosed or contained" (Ahmed, *Cultural Politics* 70). Fear of rape, for instance, is mobilised to restrict women's movement in the public sphere, as well as simultaneously securing a sense of privilege for gender normative straight men. Ahmed's work suggests that the spaces we inhabit therefore are gendered, raced, heterosexualised, and so on, and work precisely through affective channels. As we have seen, expressions of affect—disgust at the inhumanity, at an indeterminacy of trans bodies affixed at the same time—are mobilized in the courts, in the media, to produce those spaces *as* cissexual.

Arguably, a discourse of the aberrant works to secure conceptions of the community as organically whole. As Ahmed says apropos of Neighbourhood Watch programs: "the 'suspicious person' and 'the stranger' are intimately linked: they are both emptied of any content, or any direct relationship to a referent, precisely as they are tied to a (missing) history of seeing and hearing others: *they are both already seen and heard as 'the uncommon' which allows 'the common' to take its shape*" (Ahmed, *Strange Encounters* 29). Emptied of content as it is, the stranger's "strangeness" is nevertheless visually coded, the "uncommon" bodies against which normatively gendered and raced subjects construct themselves. To the degree that they do not "pass" as one gender or the other, transsexual and transgender bodies are strange, the bodies of the strangers through which the communal "we" is constituted. So the strange, the monstrous, the indeterminate are rhetorical figures that come to be inhabited by material people, occasionally as with Susan Stryker taken up and refigured subversively, but overwhelmingly, wielded against already vulnerable groups of people.

Consider Andrade's "gay things need to die" once more then, a statement apparently made about a "gay" dying cell phone battery that becomes "stuck" (to use Ahmed's terminology) to Zapata's body through their repetition together. What does its repetition shorn of context in the media do? I think it offers itself up as both a prescriptive call to cissexual action—"need"—as well as an ominous warning addressing itself to trans people. Hate speech, as Judith Butler has reminded us, addresses itself to communities, and interpellates their members into the abjected position, an individualized but collective cultural monstrosity outside of the social. When bodies known to be transsexual elicit disgust, when they are mis and ungendered, it forms a community whose borders are sealed by transphobia and homophobia. To be "it," to be a "gay thing," on the other hand, is to invite death. Between disgust and indeterminacy, the trans bodies of Angie Zapata, Sanesha Stewart, and the countless other gender variant people murdered every year have the very cultural logics that lead to their deaths repeated and confirmed by the reporting of their deaths.

NOTES

1. My thanks to Helen, Lisa, Jonathon and the other numerous transsexual, transgendered and genderqueer people whose thoughts in conversation I've benefited from.

2. Both statements were reported widely. See, for instance, Whaley's article "Smile Called 'Provoking Act' in Transgender Case" in *The Denver Post.*

3. This verdict occurred as this paper was undergoing final revisions. See Frosch's "Murder and Hate Crime verdict in Transgender Murder."

4. Here I follow Viviane Namaste's usage in *Invisible Lives,* in which she argues convincingly that while there is good reason to consider transsexual and transgender lives and politics together, many transsexual issues depart from the vaguer transgender umbrella. Further, some transsexual people resent being positioned as transgendered rather than transsexual, or indeed identify simply male or female.

5. This certainly applies to the assumptions at work in the Sanesha Stewart case, but is a common theme for many murdered trans women. It should be noted this is an assumption also shared by sensationalist news reporting in the UK—see for instance, coverage of the Kellie Telesford case in the *Croydon Today,* "Thornton Heath transsexual dies in 'kinky sex game,' Court Hears."

6. The term cis derives from its usage in chemistry, meaning "the same side as."

7. This confession is likely to have been untrue—during the trial, the prosecution argued that Andrade accompanied Zapata to a court date for a traffic date two days before her murder where her name was read as "Justin Zapata" (see Dunn, "Angie Zapata's friends"). Though as with the Stewart story, the "trans panic" defence appears to have been a fabrication, that an admitted sexual assault was unremarked upon is nevertheless extremely telling.

8. A transvestite is a person who dresses in the clothes of the other gender—in popular parlance, usually a man dressed as a woman. This is inappropriate to describe a trans woman, who is a *woman* usually dressed as a woman.

9. The story was later retitled "Ex-con Slays Transsexual 'Hooker'" on the *Daily News* website after a complaint from GLAAD.

10. Although some states do not *ever* allow transsexual men and women to change the sex marker on their birth certificates, the vast majority of regions require either a vaginoplasty (for trans women) and a hysterectomy (for trans men). The appearance and utility of trans genitals is apparently a pressing necessity for granting a change in paperwork.

11. Although it is beyond the scope of this paper to consider exactly why he was found guilty, Andrade's recent conviction may itself be partly the legacy of two things. First, his presence at court two days before with Zapata that made the trans

panic narrative extremely unlikely, and second, the queering of his ostensible heterosexuality—Andrade was found to have been cruising the bisexual area of social networking site Mocospace, and his DNA "of an intimate area" was found on a vibrator in Zapata's apartment (Dunn, "Angie Zapata's friends"). While Andrade's defense's tactic of ungendering Angie Zapata clearly appealed to transphobia and homophobia, ironically homophobia may have also contributed to his conviction. The end result of this is that the "trans panic" frame is likely to remain intact, it is merely that Andrade was proved to have *not* been surprised by Zapata's transness (and therefore trans panic was not relevant).

BIBLIOGRAPHY

Ahmed, Sara. *Strange Encounters: Embodied Others in Post-Coloniality*. London: Routledge, 2000.

———. *The Cultural Politics of Emotion*. Edinburgh: Edinburgh UP, 2004.

Anonymous. "Thornton Heath Transsexual Dies in 'Kinky Sex Game,' Court Hears." *Croydon Today*. 8 August, 2008.<http://www.thisiscroydontoday.co.uk/courts/Thornton-Heath-transsexual-died-kinky-sex-game-court-hears/article-257726-detail/article.html>.

Bettcher, Talia Mae. "Evil Deceivers and Make-Believers: On Transphobic Violence and the Politics of Illusion." *Hypatia* 22.3 (2007): 43–65.

Butler, Judith. *Excitable Speech: A Politics of the Performative*. New York: Routledge, 1997.

Cohen, Jeffrey Jerome. "Monster Theory (Seven Theses)." *Monster Theory*. Ed. Jeffrey Jerome Cohen. Minneapolis: University of Minnesota Press, 1996.

Currah, Paisley. "Expecting Bodies: The Pregnant Man and Transgender Exclusion from the Employment Non-Discrimination Act." *WSQ: Women's Studies Quarterly*. 36.3&4 (2008): 330–36.

Dunn, Sharon. "Andrade's Murder Confession Thrown Out." *Greeley Tribune*. 12 March 2009.<http://www.greeleytribune.com/article/20090312/NEWS/903119939&parentprofile=search>.

———. "Angie Zapata's friends, family take stand." *Greeley Tribune*. 18 April 2009.<http://www.greeleytribune.com/article/20090418/NEWS/904189952/1051/rss>.

Frosch, Dan. "Murder and Hate Crime Verdict in Transgender Trial." *The New York Times*. April 22 2009.<http://www.nytimes.com/2009/04/23/us/23transgend.html?_ r=1>.

Halberstam, Judith. *Skin Shows: Gothic Horror and the Technology of Monsters*. Durham: Duke UP, 1995.

Hayes, Elisabeth and Jonathon Lemire. "Ex-con Slays Transsexual 'Hooker'." *The New York Daily News*. 10 February 2008.<http://www.nydailynews.com/news/ny_crime/ 2008/02/10/2008-02-10_cops_excon_slays_bronx_transsexual_hooke.html>.

Ingebretson, Edward J. *At Stake: Monsters and the Rhetoric of Fear in Public Culture*. Chicago: Chicago UP, 2001.

Kristeva, Julia. *Powers of Horror: An Essay on Abjection*. Trans. Leon S. Roudiez. New York: Columbia UP, 1982.

Mackenzie, Gordene Olga. *Transgender Nation*. Bowling Green: Bowling Green UP, 1994.

Miller, William Ian. *The Anatomy of Disgust*. Cambridge: Harvard UP, 1997.

Moore, Tina. "Ex-con Who Stabbed Transgendered Prostitute Knew She Was a He?" *The NewYork Daily News*.12 March 2008.<http://www.nydailynews.com/news/ny_crime /2008/02/12/2008-02-12_excon_who_stabbed_transgendered_prostitu .html>.

Namaste, Viviane K. *Invisible Lives: The Erasure of Transsexual and Transgendered People*. Chicago: Chicago UP, 2000.

———. *Sex Change, Social Change: Reflections on Identity, Institutions and Imperialism*. Toronto: Women's, 2005.

Peters, Mike. "Judge to Rule on Confession in Zapata Killing." *Greeley Tribune*. 7 March 2009.<http://greeleytribune.com/article/20090307/NEWS/90306986>.

Prosser, Jay. *Second Skins: The Body Narratives of Transsexuality*. New York: Columbia UP, 1998.

Serano, Julia. *Whipping Girl: A Transsexual Woman on Sexism and the Scapegoating of Femininity*. Emeryville: Seal, 2007.

Sharpe, Andrew. *Transgender Jurisprudence: Dysphoric Bodies of Law*. London: Cavendish, 2002.

Stryker, Susan. "My Words To Victor Frankenstein Above the Village of Chamounix—Performing Transgender Rage." *Transsexual Women's Resources*. 1999.<http://www.annelawrence.com/twr/mywords.html>.

Whaley, Monte. "Smile Called 'Provoking Act' in Transgender Case." *The Denver Post*. 19 September 2008.<http://denverpost.com/breakingnews/ci_10502943>.

———. "Transgender Girl's Looks Sparked School Fight." *The Denver Post*. 28 September 2008.<http://denverpost.com/breakingnews/ci_10580442>.

———. "Court Date Set in Greeley Transgender Murder." *The Denver Post*.12 March 2008.<http://www.denverpost.com/news/ci_10308133>.

4

"A New Hope": The Psychic Life of Passing

C. Riley Snorton

> "The essence of transsexualism is the act of passing . . . I could not ask a transsexual for anything more inconceivable than to forgo passing, to be consciously "read," to read oneself aloud—and by this troubling and productive reading to begin to write oneself into the discourses by which one has been written—in effect then to become a (look out—dare I say it again?) posttransexual."
>
> —Sandy Stone, The "Empire" Strikes Back: A Posttranssexual Manifesto

> "There is no way to be(come) a human subject without recourse to the practices/readings intrinsic to most understandings of passing—that is, except by passing through passing itself."
>
> —John L. Jackson and Martha S. Jones, "Passed Performances: An Introduction"

In her groundbreaking essay, "The 'Empire' Strikes Back: A Posttranssexual Manifesto," Sandy Stone examines the contradictory implications borne out of the clinicization of transsexuality. On the one hand, Stone demonstrates the ways in which transsexuals subvert medical and psychological discourses through self-consciously, and sometimes ironically, performing scripts of gender normativity in order to receive desired "treatment." As an example, Stone focuses on the ceremonial "wringing of the chicken" in the clinic restroom—a euphemism for masturbating before surgery—as an act of multilayered recognition and medical subversion. On the other hand, Stone critiques the degree to which transsexuals deny pre-operative (MTF bottom surgery) subjectivities. By doing so, Stone warns, transsexuals maintain medico-legal discourses' narrative hold on transsexual bodies, which she defines as "a tactile politics of reproduction constituted through textual violence. The clinic is a technology of inscription" (Stone 164).

For Stone, each narrative about transsexuality—"autobiographic, academic, or clinical"—is morally inflected as it attempts to provide an authoritative explanation for the present and a mandate for the future (Stone 163). Reflecting on the relationship between language and identity, Ellie Ragland-Sullivan writes that "a gender identity maintains the desire from which the individual and social reconstitute themselves structurally as metaphors. That is, persons can speak only because language is always already a substitute that refers to something else, the desire that gives rise to speech" (Ragland-Sullivan 51). Ragland-Sullivan's conceptualization of identity as metaphor underscores Stone's urgent political question and her call for a counter-discourse. But also implicit in Stone's request for a counter-discourse is the desire for transsexuals to generate a narrative that resists the cultural imperative to pass. Stone writes: "For a transsexual, as a transsexual, to generate a true, effective and representational counterdiscourse is to speak from outside the boundaries of gender, beyond the constructed oppositional nodes which have been predefined as the only positions from which discourse is possible. How, then, can the transsexual speak? If the transsexual were to speak, what would s/he say?" (Stone 164). The question of what transsexuals would say (if they were to speak) is inflected by broader matrixes of identity and desire. The need for a counter-discourse, therefore, and attention to the writing and (proper) reading of transsexuals raise fundamental questions about desirable transsexual subjectivities, ones that resist misrecognition, which for Stone might be the instances where transsexuals are misrecognized as cisgender (or non-transgender). But Stone's articulations fail to think through the productive force of misrecognition and passing at the psychic level. Even though the psyche is simply another discursively produced site among an array of other technologies of the self, paying attention to the psychic dimensions of passing opens up new modes of thinking about the materiality of transsexual bodies.

For Stone, transsexuals who deny the "destabilizing power of being 'read' are incapable of authentic relationships, because their relationships begin as 'lies'" (Stone 167). Stone therefore argues that in order to resist a "necessity for passing . . . transsexuals must take responsibility for all of their history, to begin to rearticulate their lives not as a series of erasures in the service of a species of feminism conceived from within a traditional frame, but as a political action begun by reappropriating difference and reclaiming the power of the refigured and reinscribed body" (167). However, Stone's discussion of passing relies on a particular understanding of a post-operative transsexual body that implies that passing, even for trans people who have undergone surgeries, is a possibility that does not always already comprise a version of failure.

As Stone's manifesto evidences, passing is conventionally understood as the practice of moving from an oppressed group to a dominant group, that is, from black to white, female to male, transgender to cisgender. This "passing to privilege" narrative has animated much discussion in critical race theory and gender studies, and an extensive literature in both disciplines examines the logic of passing and its relation to identity politics. Amy Robinson writes, "The 'problem' of identity, a problem to which passing owes the very possibility of its practice, is predicated on the false promise of the visible as an epistemological guarantee" (Robinson 716). In other words, passing confounds our visually privileging cultural logic. It confuses the real with the artifice, and often even after a careful social excavation, it is hard to determine which is what. This plus its explicit relation to power is what makes passing so fascinating. And while many scholars have paid attention to the political, cultural, and even technological (medical among others) contexts that give rise to the occasion of passing, the psychological dimension of passing has remained under-theorized such that scholars have yet to examine how passing engages the psychic imagination of self.[1]

The relationship among passing, theories of sex/gender performativity, and racial practices must be considered in terms of social reading, physical embodiment, and psychic affirmation (or disavowal). A deeper consideration of the psychic life of passing requires an exploration of the interstitial relationships among articulation (we are who we say we are), performance (we are what we do), and practice (we are routinized bodily actions). In this essay I employ an auto-ethnographical approach and highlight my day-to-day experiences as a recent transplant to Philadelphia; a graduate student at the University of Pennsylvania; a black non-op, no-hormone transsexual; and a resident of rapidly gentrifying and gentrified West Philadelphia. I argue, by presenting examples of the myriad ways I pass everyday, that the psychic act of passing is an essential part of what it means to know myself. By highlighting the psychic dimensions of passing from the position of the "one who passes," I hope to emphasize its processual aspects and constitutive power, both in its ability to rearticulate social relations and to shape the contours of lived experiences. Although passing has traditionally been considered in one of three forms—a ploy for power, a lie, or a form of misrecognition—focusing on its psychic components may help to reform our understanding of passing such that we value it as the function by which one distinguishes oneself as a human subject (Jackson and Jones 11).

This chapter, like Stone's, is interested in questions of narrativity and the contexts, origins, and possibilities of speech regarding transsexuality. It is also preoccupied with concepts like hope, dreams, possibilities, aspirations, realities, and resignations, and to that end attempts to think through the interdependency of these terms as they relate to transsexuality, transgender studies, and (dare I say it) gender liberation. In contrast to Stone's call for truthful and representative counter-narratives, I explore the ways in which popular and academic discourses about passing render non-operative, no-hormone transsexuals illegible in conversations about transsexuality. Looking particularly at the work of Jay Prosser, Judith Butler, and Stone, I examine how discussions of transsexuality often presume a corporeal materiality that does not aptly characterize the lived experiences of transsexuals who are not able to pass in a traditional sense. This chapter hopes to complicate and expand definitions of transsexuality and passing through a serious investigation of the political and personal investments in concepts such as "the psyche" and "hope," and their relation to transsexual embodiment. In the first of the three sections, I examine the literature on transsexuality and its relation to narrative form to discuss the disjunctures that arise when theory takes autobiography as its primary material or data. In the second section, I recount a personal experience with passing in my neighborhood barbershop to highlight the ways in which academic discourses about passing and transsexuality rarely reference black, non-operative, no-hormone transsexual bodies. In the final part, I turn to the political possibilities for trans people when passing is no longer primarily defined as a deceitful practice. Drawing on the work of Vincent Crapanzano and Cornel West, this paper seeks to find "a new hope" (to use another *Star Wars* reference) for those who pass.

PASSING AND LEGIBILITY: WHAT BELIES THE BODY AND TEXT

Scholars who write about transsexuality have rightly paid a great deal of attention to the ways transsexuals talk about their bodies and the relation between speech and embodiment. In his book *Second Skins*, Jay Prosser writes, "a body narrative is the story the transsexual weaves around the body in order that this body may be 'read'" (Prosser 101). For Prosser, the "second" sexing of the transsexual body is constituted by narrative, in which "transsexuality [serves] as a passage through space, a journey from one location to another" (5). He writes: "In this sense transition serves as a key means by which transsexuals represent their relations not only to gendered belonging but to sexual communities and politics (lesbian, gay, straight, queer, and, most recently, transgendered)" (5). Employing Didier Anzieu's concept of the "skin ego" while taking Butler to task for her theories of gender performativity, Prosser contends that transsexuals experience their bodies as beyond their physical contours or dimensions; as certain contours are unincorporable into their self-images, others that are not yet corporeal are felt to be present. He then provides a list of physical transformations that transsexuals undergo. However, in referring to physical transformation as a transsexual's "life quest," he fails to reflect on the large number of transsexuals for whom a different corporeality never (fully) materializes (Prosser 67).

Arguing primarily against earlier writings (and readings) of Butler, Prosser argues that *Gender Trouble* enables the syllogism "transgender = gender performativity = queer = subversive" (Prosser 33). Prosser contends that transsexed people become transsexed to themselves from within their bodily experience, whereas they become transsexed to others through the mechanisms of being able to tell a narrative, which can be believed as a justification for being transsexed. For Prosser, the narrative, found particularly in the form of autobiography, provides the "means to passing through transsexuality and to passing back into it" (131). However, this argument, like Stone's thesis in "Empire," fails to conceptualize pre-operative and non-operative transsexual bodies. Moreover, it is fundamentally unclear what precisely is meant by "bodily experience," as one's experience of one's body is filtered through the mind. An experience of the body therefore must be at least partially psychically determined, and while it is true that a different body can constitute a different sense of self, it is not the only way in which transsexuals understand themselves. However, the legibility of Prosser's transsexual subjects is not only inscribed on the page through their autobiographies, but perhaps more importantly, it is written on the body. Prosser explicitly states that the people he describes are all writing post-operatively (by which he refers to MTF bottom surgery), but what happens when the pre-operative or non-operative transsexual wants to write her own narrative too? How might that story contribute and alter existing discourses on sexuality? What happens when the story of the transsexual body does not evidence a clear break from a sexual ontological past?

Throughout her career and particularly in *Undoing Gender*, Judith Butler has offered new (revised) frameworks with which to understand the cultural legibility of transgender people in society. In *Undoing Gender*, Butler argues that one is always performing gender for an "other," even if that other is imaginary (Butler 32). For Butler, gender is a social relation in which no one person can be the author of her own gender. Drawing on Hegel, she makes the link between desire and recognition when she writes, "But if the schemes of recognition that are available to us are those that 'undo' the person by conferring recognition or 'undo' the person by withholding recognition, then recognition becomes a site of power by which the human is differentially produced" (4). Therefore recognition, partly borrowing from Foucault's concept of subjectivation,[2] is informed by social norms that are not chosen and that serve as the proof of one's agency.

In *Undoing Gender*, Butler frames transgender legibility within a discourse about "conflict." She rightly attends to the heightened manner with which transgender and transsexual people of color are subject to pathologization and violence, often as a result of being read on the streets as trans. Butler also elucidates an interesting paradox, which is the substance of subjectivation, in which the questions of autonomy and self-determination are bound by institutions that "are laid out in advance and prior to one's choice," and "conversely (and as a consequence) it turns out that changing the institutions by which humanly visible choice is established and maintained is a prerequisite for the exercise of self-determination" (Butler 7). Although the irony Butler describes, that is, that our subjectivities are produced by structures that seek to constrain us, is resonant with the experiences of transsexuals and people more generally, the relation between what is human and what is visible/legible is problematic as it seems to preclude the possibilities for other communities to validate the lives of those who may be culturally illegible elsewhere. For example, pre- and non-operative, no-hormone transsexuals may find legibility among friends, family, support groups, and other trans people. They may also find recognition in their own minds.

Moreover, the lack of distinction between what is human and socially legible obscures her argument, which suggests that sometimes one's social audience can be imaginary. While the social plays an important role in framing our understanding of "self," cultural and social legibility cannot predetermine what is human in every sense; there must be space for the "psyche" or the staging of self for our imaginary other in self-determination as well. We are human, even if it is simply because we imagine ourselves to be. Similarly, the social illegibility of a heteronormatively gendered queer person (for example, a lesbian who is read as straight) or an Anglo-looking person of color may be the very condition that produces a form of psychic legibility evidenced by the experience of cognitive dissonance on the part of the one who passes. Misrecognition, therefore, is as important as recognition in the production of self, as the quality of feeling misrecognized/unseen/wrongly viewed serves as a context for the emergence of selfhood. The sense of feeling misrecognized also serves as a site for resistance in forms of identification governed by the politics of recognition, as the possibility of misrecognition carries with it the opportunity for deliberation and the potential rejection of social scripts, which get mapped onto one's body.

In "Male Lesbians and the Postmodern Body," Jacquelyn N. Zita examines the ways "male lesbians" are made possible and recognizable by postmodern discourse. In her exploration of how postmodernism opens up space for new sexualities and genders, Zita outlines four strategies "male lesbians" could employ to gain membership in lesbian spaces or to be legible as lesbian: 1) a "post-operative transsexual" strategy, in which one changes one's secondary sexual characteristics; 2) a "transgendering" strategy, where one asks those around one to see one's "inner" self; 3) a "genital de-essentializing" strategy, where one asks people to dissociate one's genital from one's sexual identification; and 4) a "genderfuck" strategy, in which one would participate in sexual acts of the opposite sex (Zita 118–19).

However, Zita vehemently rejects passing as a strategy, either within the "charmed circle" of the lesbian space (in which she doesn't seem to believe that a male lesbian could "pass") or in the outside "straight world." She points to the inevitable failure to pass as a justification to exclude passing from the ranks of postmodern strategies when she writes,

> [W]hen our "male lesbian" fails to maintain a consistent female identity at all times, this is not a failure in postmodern imagination but an indication of the individual's inability to control over-determined hegemonic readings from the outside world forced on the body. When these readings numerically outnumber the less frequent "lesbian" attribution in the charmed circle, this external world definitely "sexes" his body. (125)

Zita goes as far as to suggest that a numerical outnumbering of attributions as male over lesbian serves to "sex" the body of the male lesbian. What is absent in her discussion, however, is any sort of "male lesbian" interiority. The critical question remains, what allows for a male-bodied lesbian to continue understanding herself as lesbian even in the face of constant misrecognition? This is the question I attempt to address in a discussion of my barbershop experiences as a FTM transsexual (often read as female).

In telling my own story, I recognize that I am met with the same predicament as others who have written on transsexuality—namely privileging autobiographical/autoethnographical data as a means to create theory. However, I find it impossible to discuss the relations between narrativity and embodiment, speech and legibility, passing and hope without explicitly describing how these ideas are informed by my experiences as a black, non-operative, no-hormone transsexual. Part of what readers might notice is the dramatic change in tone, an emphasis on thick description over theoretical moves. In this shift, I hope to at least characterize the disjunctures between theory and everyday narratives about transsexuality. Particularly as it relates to passing, I offer (borrowing from Harold Garfinkel[3]) that contextualizing passing as a practice within the daily routines of non-operative, no-hormone transsexuals requires moving beyond the clinic as the primary site of inscription such that we recognize passing as enabled as much by technologies of the mind as those of the body. Passing, as a mental narrative, then gets precisely at the heart of the questions that animate discussions about transsexuality—namely how does one articulate oneself as transsexual?

TAKING A STOP BY THE BARBERSHOP: A QUOTIDIAN AUTOETHNOGRAPHY[4]

A couple of years ago I moved to West Philadelphia to begin graduate studies at the University of Pennsylvania. Early on I looked for a barbershop to continue my twice-a-month shape-up ritual. Less than one block from my house I found three barbershops all located about two or three storefronts away from one particular corner. I immediately nixed Tony's Barbershop, whose tagline reads "Just for Men," as a viable option since I felt sure that the man I know myself to be would not necessarily reflect the man Tony or his clients had in mind. The other two shops, The Hair Lounge and Natural Impressions, remain the two barbershops I frequent in order to maintain a fresh cut.

Between a Chinese-run American deli and a bar that appears to be open sixteen hours a day is a fairly small shop called The Hair Lounge. Three barber chairs line the left side of the shop with about ten seats for waiting on the opposite side of the narrow space. At the end of the room, opposite the door, is a twenty-six-inch TV tuned usually to Jerry Springer or Maury Povich during the day or to the news in the evening. This is the shop I prefer, as the television has provided me with solace in the last twenty-eight months I have been patronizing this shop. Natural Impressions, my alternate barbershop, has had a broken window for over a year. This even smaller shop also has three barber's chairs, but only two barbers are ever present. Five or six chairs for waiting face the barber's seats. There is no working TV, only a small radio perched on a bench covered with magazines, newspapers, and the remaining stray shards of the broken glass from the storefront window.

These three barbershops, in such close proximity to one another, thrive on very different clientele. Tony's caters mostly to men over forty. Urban legend has it that Tony's used to serve as a spot for exotic dancers, hence the "for men only" also speaks to the historical, homosocial practice of watching female exotic dancers. The Hair Lounge, which is definitely the most popular of the three shops, is frequented mostly by young African American men in their twenties but also by children and some women (one of the barbers also threads eyebrows). Natural Impressions has an almost exclusively immigrant patronage, mostly Haitian and West African.

The very first time I stepped into The Hair Lounge, I was misrecognized for one patron's friend—a friend he knew from the bar next door. As the man proceeded to share with me some inside joke between himself and his friend, I became acutely aware of the palpable tension rising in the atmosphere of the shop. My barber, Slopes, and another barber exchanged confused glances, not simply because I was not this man's bar mate but because they read my gender as female. The man stopped his story abruptly, and I began to feel so anxious as to excuse myself from the shop by saying in the lowest possible voice I could muster that I was going next door to the deli to get some iced tea. When I returned five minutes later all the barbers began to apologize profusely for what had happened. I told them there was nothing to apologize about, but they didn't seem to understand my intended meaning. The man who at first was interested in sharing a joke and a laugh rather embarrassedly excused himself from the shop. I can only assume that in the time it took to grab a bottled beverage, deliberation took place and consensus was reached on my often multiply read, "indecipherable" gender expression.

Through consensus, I became a female in the barbershop, yet at the same time each succeeding visit has shown that the process has never been fully "complete." One Friday afternoon during Maury Povich I sat down in Slopes's chair after the requisite hour-and-a-half wait to see which of Povich's formulas would air that day. The show featured updates on his "wildest" previous guests. Most times in the shop, when the TV is on, light banter takes precedence over the background noise of the daytime talk shows. However, when a segment came on about a black trans woman and sex worker who on a previous episode came out as transgender to her mother and sister, the barbershop was uneasily silent. As I sat in the chair, I pretended to keep my eyes on the television screen. However, I could not help trying to survey the room, perhaps because I am always trying to practice the art of ethnography, but most certainly because I wanted to assess my level of danger. As my eyes darted around the room, I saw the other patrons once rapt in conversation now pretending to listen intently to the segment while practicing their own careful surveying of me and the effeminate, presumably gay man who sat exactly opposite me cross-legged in tight jeans. I too looked at the man I read as queer, hoping to make eye contact and share an imperceptible nod of recognition. However, there was none to be made, no solidarity had, and at virtually the same instant I realized we were all practicing a form of reading (of looking but not seeing) to help us through this moment of quiet crisis.

Our social drama continued even after Povich wrapped up the segment, promising to keep us updated on the woman's progress, when the show cut to a commercial break, and the man seated in the barber's chair next to me uttered the first phrase since the segment had come on: "We don't need to see any more about that. Please don't keep me updated on what's going on with him." The barbershop filled with laughter. On one level this patron's comments could simply be read as homophobic and transphobic and dismissed out of hand. However, that would overlook the productive value not only of the comment but of the ensuing laughter. It is important to note that every single person in the barbershop laughed, of course presumably not for the same reasons. But the collective laughter served as a productive site for an articulation of a form of black masculinity, marked by an acute sense of precariousness and the need for performative recuperation.

E. Patrick Johnson, in his discussion about the relationship between race and performance, cites Clifford Geertz in describing the interactions between black researchers and researched as a "fragile fiction" (Johnson 10). For Johnson, "fragile fiction" describes the mental and literary narratives ethnographers create to account for time in the field (10). Surely this helps to explain my experiences in the barbershop: a black researcher interested in the production of my gender in social space. However, it seems also to aptly describe an aspect of black masculinity more generally. In his larger project, Johnson critically examines discourses of black masculinity and tropes of authenticity to argue for appropriative performances of blackness as a means to undermine and subvert dominant scripts of black masculinity. Johnson writes, "blackness does not only reside in theatrical fantasy of the white imaginary that is then projected onto black bodies, nor is it always consciously acted out; rather, it is also the inexpressible yet undeniable racial experience of black people" (8). In this way, the barbershop laughter, robust and polysemic, signifies a moment of synthesis in what Victor Turner might have described as a symbolic ritual of masculinity. However, the literature on passing and transsexuality rarely takes into account the experiences of transgender people with multiple identities, particularly trans people of color, such that a person who passes as a black man both to himself and others is not typically vested with the keys to patriarchal authority but rather is engaged constantly in elaborate rituals of recuperation as a person of color, as a transgender person, as an assemblage of identifications.

Wrapped in my reflections, I felt particularly uneasy on my half-block walk back from the barbershop to my apartment. In many ways, the woman on the screen mirrored back to me a version of the person I know myself to be: a black body, misread, spectacularized, and often confusing to others. I laughed when everybody else did, not because I didn't care to hear about her ongoing struggles with her family, but because I felt exposed. As a trans man often read as a little boy or a butch lesbian, I often confront the "failure" of my masculinity—one that I understand as both queer and male. For the men in the barbershop, the trans woman materialized the specter of compromised black masculinity, her gender presentation marked (like my own) by her non-operative, no-hormone status.

In his *Imagining Transgender*, David Valentine studies mostly MTF transsexuals who identify as women but who also maintain strong ties to gay male culture. For Valentine, his informants live at the interstices of distinct and separable genders and sexualities and elucidate how categories such as "transgender or homosexuality [are] a modern and recent innovation" (Valentine 169). Like those of Valentine's informants, my experiences in my sexed body and transsexed mind require new articulations of theories of the psychic dimensions of transsexuality. Generally, the presence of non-operative, no-hormone transsexuals problematizes the relationship between transsexuality and medical narratives such that the relationship between power and passing is more fluid, situational, and culturally inflected; these occasions can and often do operate outside of the clinic to take place at the barbershop, grocery store, and other informal spaces of social gathering.

Shifting the focus of transsexual theory away from discourses of medicalization necessarily requires broadening traditional definitions of passing. For the vast majority of transsexuals who are not able to "pass" all the time, passing is not simply a question of how one is read but includes an agential power of affirming one's own reading of self. Definitions of passing therefore must also include its psychological function, that is, that it brings one's "self" into view. Through the experiences of psychic dissonance, affirmation, disavowal, and recognition, we engage in the process of passing off our daily experiences of embodiment as identifications—creating "fragile fictions" of personhood. Therefore passing is not simply the essence of transsexualism; it is the way we make identity. An expansion of passing to include its psychic dimension opens up new possibilities for thinking about all kinds of bodies, identities, and performances. And for non-operative, no-hormone transsexuals, a broader definition of passing is key to the psychic survival of trans people who are not read as the gender they prefer all the time (which may be every trans person). Passing, then, may be the mechanism by which Zita's "male" lesbians sustain a sense of their identity amid constant misrecognition, as it is the way I continue to live in community in West Philadelphia.

This is not to suggest that transsexuals and particularly transsexuals of color are not susceptible to physical and structural violence prompted by the readings and misreadings of their bodies. Peggy Phelan, in concert with Butler, acknowledges that the risks of visibility—a product of passing—for transsexuals may lead to sexual violence, assault, and murder. For Phelan, passing is a narrative about visibility and the risks of translation: "The risk of visibility then is the risk of any translation—a weaker version of the original script, the appropriation by (economically and artistically) powerful 'others'" (Phelan 97). Therefore, passing is sometimes politically and culturally necessary to avoid misrepresentation, and more importantly, physical harm. However, I would offer that an examination of the psychic dimensions of passing, which allows for the possibilities of productive misrecognition and internal deliberation, is necessary for the avoidance of psychological harm. On the numerous occasions where I am read as a cisgender woman, passing becomes a necessary mechanism to understand these situations as not simply a failure to present as the gender I recognize myself to be, but also as instances of passing. These moments of passing (of visibility and misrecognition) for a woman become the substance (a process of dissonance and disidentification) of my own psychic recognition as a trans man.

Misrecognition structures social identifications, as Walter Benn Michaels argues, with regard to the social construction of race. For Michaels, social understandings of race always contain some form of "misrecognition of biology" (Michaels 411). Arguing against social constructionists who argue that there is no material reality to racial identity, Michaels contends that if identity is "nothing but a distinctive array of beliefs and practices, then there could be no such thing as passing, since to believe and practice what the members of any race [or identity group] believed and practiced would, by definition, make you a member of that race [or identity]" (411). As he rightly points out, there must be something other than performance that constitutes the reading of identity, which in the case of race might be physically (or even phenotypically) marked. However, it is also useful to think about Michaels's theory in the obverse, such that our psychic investment in race, gender, and so on is predicated upon our grouping together beliefs and cultural practices and "passing them off" as identity. In other words, part of the process of identification might be aptly described as a form of passing. Broadening Prosser's formulation, identifications are formed by passing through identity and passing back into it.

THE POSSIBILITY OF A NEW HOPE

The title of this chapter "A New Hope" is partly in response to Stone's "The Empire Strikes Back," as it takes the prequel movie in the *Star Wars* series to illustrate the recuperative qualities of passing for non-operative, no-hormone transsexuals. However, it is also informed by theories about hope. Concepts like "hope" and "psyche" are both vested with meanings that transcend any recourse to base materialism. One cannot find these concepts in the material world, for they evoke the ritualistic and perhaps even spiritual investments we have in humanity. In the wake of a presidential election where hope was deployed as a rallying call to vote, hope as an idea took on an explicitly political edge, as it stood in for the possibility of change in the midst of a tremendous financial crisis and an ongoing "war on terror." As President Barack Obama states in his *New York Times* bestseller, it is the position we must take when "we have no choice" (Obama 8). Hope, however, does not simply spring eternal from the shared values of the American citizenry, as Obama might have us imagine. Nor can it simply be a "rhetoric of deflection," a means to defer action until some unforeseen future (Crapanzano 8). Rather, hope is an orientation toward politics (cultural, electoral, and otherwise), which demonstrates a willingness to engage, even as it seems hopelessly naïve to do so. As an analytic, hope rightly attends to the psychosocial construction of reality while also forcing us to contend with the political and personal investments we have in belonging, recognition, and legibility. Like passing, hope might also expand our understanding of transsexual bodies as it places the material (the physical body) and immaterial (the psyche) in productive tension.

Cornel West's *Hope on a Tightrope: Words and Wisdom* explicitly engages the politics of hope when he argues that "real hope is grounded in a particularly messy struggle and it can be betrayed by naïve projections of a better future that ignore the necessity of doing the real work" (West 6). Distinguishing hope from optimism, which he described in a public lecture as "[adopting] the role of the spectator who surveys the evidence in order to infer that things are going to get better," West argues that in this time, people must arm themselves with hope to confront the overwhelming currents of inequality, global capitalism, social breakdown, and personal disillusionment; it is "what keeps us sane" (West 2005). West's connection of psychological well-being with his politically inflected definition of hope is critical to my understanding of the relationship between hope and passing. For transsexuals like me, passing is a hopeful stance that sustains an ability to articulate a transsexual identity in the face of discourses of clinicization and social misreading. Passing, like hope, keeps me sane, or at least helps me cope in an environment that does not produce the identity I psychically inhabit.

However, more so than their restorative psychological value, theories of hope also intervene in conversations about the materiality of transsexual bodies. Crapanzano, in his "Reflections on Hope as a Category of Social and Psychological Analysis," writes that hope is "intimately linked to desire," such that meanings of hope and desire may overlap when the length of time is short, or hope can become a passive counterpart to desire when the duration of time is indefinite (Crapanzano 7). In this idea of hope lies an aspirational future that implicates individual practice in the present (25). In other words, hope casts the present in a historical light. As Jurgen Moltmann argues in *The Theology of Hope*, hope takes seriously the possibilities with which "all reality is fraught" (Moltmann 25). Hope for understanding non-operative, no-hormone transsexuals might be restored through an understanding of passing that does not rely exclusively on the "reality" of the materiality of the transsexual body. Instead, hope and passing create room for imagining the world differently and in doing so, for transforming the scripts of gendered embodiment. In the space outside of the clinic, passing gives way to hope for transsexuals who seek to find community and to reconcile the differences between the intersubjective but often dissonant worlds of the social and the mind.

While Crapanzano describes desire as "effective," hope is decidedly affective and "can never be fully divorced from hopelessness any more than hopelessness can be divorced from hope" (Crapanzano 17). Hope is the waking dreams, the psychic delusions, the slippery knowledge produced by passing that render legible non-operative, no-hormone transsexuals. It is not the counter-narratives Stone requires, which may in fact be "turtles all the way down," as discourses and counter-discourses are often informed by the same core values and beliefs. Rather hope, like the psychic dimensions of passing, allows for the flexibility to make claims about the body that transcend conversations about materiality. It allows for the possibility of transition, which does not occur on the surgeon's table at the clinic but instead in the spaces where people come together or in the quiet moments of reflection in one's room. Although I deeply appreciate the intervention Stone has made in her "Post-transsexual Manifesto," I hope to provide a more hopeful reading for transsexuals who "pass." If indeed passing is the essence of transsexualism, this essay seeks to explore what new possibilities are afforded when passing is explored psychically and when transsexual bodies are black and non-operative. As a response to the sets of questions this essay lays out, I offer that we should resist taking narratives of passing as clear-cut (black and/to white). Instead we must open ourselves to the productive possibilities of the "gray" and the contradictory social spaces some trans people inhabit at the edges of legibility.

However, as Butler suggests, possibility itself is a normative value. She contends, "Possibility is an aspiration, something we might hope will be equitably distributed, something that cannot be taken for granted, especially if it is apprehended phenomenologically . . . The thought of a possible life is only an indulgence for those who already know themselves to be possible. For those who are still looking to become possible, possibility is a necessity" (Butler 31). It is my hope that a more expansive definition of passing, one that takes into account its "psychic" dimensions (as a complementary or competing discursive space in theorizations about the transsexual body), helps us consider the necessity of including more voices in the discussion about transsexuality.

NOTES

Thanks to Ann Garry, Talia Bettcher, John L. Jackson, Jr., Katherine Sender, Nancy J. Hirschmann, Peggy Sanday, Zenzele Isoke, Jes Batis, and the anonymous reviewers for comments on this paper. An earlier version of this paper was presented at the Race, Sex, Power Conference in Chicago, March of 2008.

1. Marjorie Garber and Pamela Caughie both mention the psychic dimensions of passing in their work. Marjorie Garber, in her *Vested Interests: Cross Dressing and Cultural Anxieties*, discusses how the event of passing for transsexuals and transvestites create a psychic crisis for the audience such that it renders explicit the arbitrariness of the phallus. She writes, "the extraordinary power of the transvestite [is] as an aesthetic and psychological agent of destabilization, desire and fantasy" (Garber 71). Garber makes use of the psychic dimension, in many ways corroborating popular readings of Judith Butler's *Gender Trouble*. On the other hand, Pamela Caughie, in her *Passing and Pedagogy: The Dynamics of Responsibility*, wants to theorize passing from the vantage

point of the one who passes. Caughie writes that, "With passing come new anxieties about performing as 'the one supposed to know' (Lacan), which always entail the possibility of being exposed as a fraud" (Caughie 58). However, this remains a partial picture of the psychological dimension of passing by emphasizing an ontological reality that is psychically known and performatively masked.

2. In *The Psychic Life of Power,* Butler explicates her implicit use of the concept of subjectivation when she writes: "The subject is the linguistic occasion for the individual to achieve and reproduce intelligibility, the linguistic condition of its existence and agency. No individual becomes a subject without first becoming subjected [to] or undergoing 'subjectivation'. . . It makes little sense to treat 'the individual' as an intelligible term if individuals are said to acquire their intelligibility by becoming subjects. Paradoxically, no intelligible reference to individuals or their becoming can take place without a prior reference to their status as subjects. The story by which subjection is told is inevitably circular, presupposing the very subject for which it seeks to give an account" (Butler 11)

3. Garfinkel defines passing as a necessary strategy for transsexuals. He writes, "The work of achieving and making secure their rights to live in the elected sex status while providing for the possibility of detection and ruin carried out within the socially structured conditions in which this work occurred I shall call 'passing'" (Garfinkel 118). While the language of "detection" is troubling as it maintains a false distinction between the truth and the pretense of the body, Garfinkel's emphasis on the importance of social conditions in structuring the process is crucial to my own understanding of passing.

4. In a discussion of how autobiography challenges traditional anthropology's reliance on emic/etic distinctions, Michael M. J. Fischer writes, "Standing between the individual and the social, autobiography is a site of interplay between the modernist vision of autonomous bounded egos and postmodernist decentered selves" (Fischer 180). For Fischer, "identity quests are focal points for the cultural creation of a new ethos for the postmodern world" (192). In this way, autobiographies are able to make "etic" proclamations as the "frame of a life history" serves as an "experiential field" for identifying the ways in which broader historical forces intersect to articulate a subject" (192). Sue Thomas cites Mary Louise Pratt as having developed the concept autoethnography, which employs the following principle: "[i]f ethnographic texts are a means by which Europeans represent to themselves their (usually subjugated) others, autoethnographic texts are those the others construct in relation to or in dialogue with those metropolitan representations" (Thomas 9).

BIBLIOGRAPHY

Anzieu, Didier. *Skin Ego: A psychoanalytic approach to the self.* New Haven: Yale UP, 1989.

Butler, Judith. *Gender Trouble: Feminism and the subversion of identity.* New York: Routledge, 1990.

——. *The psychic life of power: Theories in subjection.* Stanford: Stanford UP, 1997.

———. *Undoing Gender*. New York: Routledge, 2004.

Caughie, *Pamela. Passing and pedagogy: The dynamics of responsibility*. Champaign: University of Illinois Press, 1999.

Crapanzano, Vincent. "Reflections on hope as a category of social and psychological analysis." *Cultural Anthropology* 18.1 (2003): 3–32.

Fischer, Michael M. J. *Emergent forms of life and the anthropological voice*. Durham: Duke UP, 2003.

Garber, Marjorie. *Vested interests: Cross dressing and cultural anxieties*. New York: Routledge, 1992.

Garfinkel, Harold. *Studies in ethnomethodology*. Englewood Cliffs: Prentice Hall, 1967.

Jackson, John, and Martha S. Jones. "Passed performances: an introduction." *Women and Performance: A Journal of Feminist Theory* 15.1 (2005): 9–17.

Johnson, E. Patrick. *Appropriating blackness: Performance and the politics of authenticity*. Durham: Duke UP, 2003.

Michaels, Walter Benn. "Critical response II: The no drop rule." *Critical Inquiry* 20.4 (1994): 758–69.

Moltmann, Jurgen. *The theology of hope*. New York: Harper and Row, 1967.

Obama, Barack. *The audacity of hope: Thoughts on reclaiming the American dream*. New York: Three Rivers, 2006.

Phelan, Peggy. *Unmarked: The politics of performance*. New York: Routledge, 1993.

Prosser, Jay. *Second skins: The body narratives of transsexuality*. New York: Columbia UP, 1998.

Ragland-Sullivan, Ellie. "The sexual masquerade: A Lacanian theory of sexual difference." *Lacan and the Subject of Language*. Ed. Ellie Ragland-Sullivan and Mark Bracher. New York: Routledge, 1991.

Robinson, Amy. "It takes one to know one: Passing and communities of common interest." *Critical Inquiry* 20.4 (1994): 715–37.

Stone, Sandy. "The 'empire' strikes back: A posttransexual manifesto." *Camera Obscura* 29 (1992): 150–76.

Thomas, Sue. *The worlding of Jean Rhys*. Westport: Greenwood, 1999.

Turner, Victor. *The ritual process: Structure and anti-structure*. Piscataway: Aldine Transaction, 1995.

Valentine, David. *Imagining transgender: an ethnography of a category*. Durham: Duke UP, 2007.

West, Cornel. "Prisoners of hope." Alternet.com. 1 Dec. 2007.<http://www.alternet.org/story/20982>.

———. *Hope on a tightrope: Words and wisdom*. New York: Smiley Books, 2008.

Zita, Jacquelyn N. "Male lesbians and the postmodern body." Hypatia 7.4 (1992): 106–27.

PART II

5

Fuck/The Police: Queering Narratives of Police Brutality in Post 9-11 New York

Marty Fink

As a queer graduate student living in New York City, I often contemplate the connections between queer theory, police brutality, and public space. By placing the works of two of my own queer heroes in dialogue with one another, I hope to show how theoretical models can help us to (at least theoretically) combat policing itself. Using *Times Square Red, Times Square Blue* to undertake a reading of Leslie Feinberg's *Stone Butch Blues,* I hope to resituate Feinberg's textual representation of policing and queer space within Delany's framework of contact. Through my engagement with Feinberg and Delany, I intend to challenge the notion that policing is an uncontested top down manifestation of power, suggesting instead that policing may in fact be reclaimed by the deviant bodies, sexualities, and even graduate students who occupy New York's public space.

In *Times Square Red, Times Square Blue,* Samuel Delany demonstrates the importance of interclass contact as a built in feature of our neighborhoods and cityscapes. Contact between persons of working and middle classes in the form of greetings, advice, suggestions, casual sex, recommendations, and commercial transactions is, Delany argues, pivotal to the functioning of a democratic society. Delany illustrates the elemental role of these relations within New York's (old) Times Square, demonstrating the ways in which the commercial development of the area is intended to eradicate the sexualized spaces and practices crucial to the enactment not only of gay male desire, but of a politically gratifying urban life. Delany undertakes a feminist analysis of danger and policing within urban areas, distinguishing between the realities of urban violence and mythical discourses held in place by the state. Self-policing, Delany shows, is a natural outcome of diverse urban planning and frequent interclass contact. Such relations allow the function of the police to be reclaimed by concerned urban residents themselves, rather than by violent and discriminatory institutional controls.

I lived in New York for about six months before I was apprehended by the NYPD and charged with a misdemeanor. When I arrived at my court date, I sat uncomfortably as an involuntary witness to the misdeeds of my fellow offenders as proclaimed by the surly Brooklyn judge—assault, cocaine use, breaking parole, refusing a drug test—until it was as last my turn. I stepped up to the side of the legal aid representative who seemed remarkably underdressed next to everyone else in a suit, and waited for the old white man to name my offense: "unleashed animal." Yes, I had to miss graduate school, take a train and a bus, face deportation and criminal charges, all for letting my dog trot freely down a secluded Prospect Park path at 3:15pm, one hour and forty-five minutes prior to the designated off-leash time. "Can't you give me a warning?" I very politely asked the cop back at the park—"I can, but I don't have to, so I'm not going to," she informed me while returning my driver's license, "and if you don't provide me with a US address, I will put you in jail." Standing in court, I became privy to the humiliating repercussions afforded to even the most innocuous transgressions of authority in New York's public space. I recalled the writings of heroes like Assata Shakur who decades ago identified the mechanisms of violence and repression that establish the city as "a minimum security prison" (60) in order to dissipate the political mobilization of people, especially Black people and people of color, within the United States. In spite of my own exposure to such texts, I did not expect to come up against police harassment so quickly by simply occupying public space in New York. I deeply missed living in the more off-the-radar Montreal where the parks were at least somewhat self-policing and if say, a dog was doing something it ought not have, other park users would speak out for or against one another, regulating their own community without facing abuse from the state. Not only were such regulations often left up to common sense, but this type of social situation allowed for a hodgepodge of neighborhood residents to interact with and often get to know one another while ignoring institutional legislations that were thought unreasonable or unkind. This random network of strangers in the park is actually an example of Delany's contact zone, an interclass community capable not only of self-regulation but of sexual gratification as well.

Delany's concept of contact, moreover, challenges the function of policing in New York City. Well designed neighborhoods, Delany argues, can be protected by "self-policing" (156), where frequent contact between residents supplants the need for violent intrusion by the police. Delany defines contact as a "broadly social" (129) phenomenon which "appears at random" (129). He attempts to pin down its illusive nature by citing some of its most emblematic occurrences: "contact is the conversation that starts in the line at the grocery counter with the person behind you while the clerk is changing the paper roll in the cash register. It is the pleasantries exchanged with a neighbor who has brought her chair out to take some air on the stoop. It is the discussion that begins with the person next to you at a bar" (123). Delany defines two further features essential to his notion of contact. Firstly, contact allows members of different classes to aid and understand one another. This feature of contact is made possible by the "public space and the architecture and commerce that depend on and promote it" (129). Architecture itself, Delany reveals, allows members of various classes and experiences to form alliances toward the enrichment of their communities. Contact, as a result, "regularly crosses class lines in those public spaces in which interclass encounters are at their most frequent" (129). Well planned space transcends lines of class distinction, allowing residents to contribute to the flow of information and activity that permeates their surroundings, participating in everything from commercial promotion to career advancement. Delany alerts us to the fact that "in a society that prides itself on the widespread existence of opportunity, interclass contacts are the site and origin of a good many of what can later be seen as life opportunities, or at least the site of many elements that make the seizing of such opportunities easier and more profitable" (156).

While Delany's observations about interclass contact and neighborly congeniality seem almost commonsensical, it is the second essential component of contact that makes Delany's theory both daring and transgressive, connecting his work in an indispensible way to that of Feinberg. Delany stipulates that:

> very importantly, contact is also the intercourse—physical and conversational—that blooms in and as "casual sex" in public rest rooms, sex movies, public parks, singles bars, and sex clubs, on street corners with heavy hustling traffic, and in the adjoining motels or the apartments of one or another participant, from which nonsexual friendships and/or acquaintances of one or another participant from which nonsexual friendships and/or acquaintances lasting for decades or a lifetime may spring. (123)

Contact thus takes on a necessarily sexual nature, which may or may not result in lasting physical and/or emotional bonds. Recognizing the desire inherent to human social interactions, as well as the sexual possibilities made available through our built environment, Delany hinges the cross-class unification of strangers to our undeniably sexual drives. Not only should public sex go unpoliced, Delany argues, it should actually be formalized and spatially encouraged, creating an environment where other behaviors such as sexual violence, drug use, and theft, could then be controlled. This control, moreover, would be enforced not by police offers, but by residents themselves. Like Mary Louise Pratt's conception of the contact zone as "social spaces where cultures meet, clash, and grapple with each other, often in contexts of highly asymmetrical relations of power, such as colonialism, slavery, or their aftermaths" (34), Delany's contact zone allows for the "point of entry" (Pratt 35) of traditionally marginalized groups into the legal discourse surrounding their lives.

I experienced these types of contact zones while living in Montreal, where various public spaces from baseball diamonds and train tracks, to skill shares and bike shops, provided opportunities for dialogue between queers. In Montreal I also enjoyed forms of social networking that Delany distinguishes from contact as being more "indoor" (129), promotional, and "motive-driven" (129). Events hosted by Montreal-based groups like the "Anticapitalist Asspirates" provided queers from around the city with an opportunity to get to know one another, but also to get it on. Dance parties in particular offered a crucial forum for women and gender variant people to express their sexualities in pubic. The Asspirates created alternative spaces to those like the aforementioned dog-walking park whose cruising grounds, while well known, cater only to men. The complete absence of women in such public sex situations was parodied by a friend of mine in a school project entitled "The Lesbian Cruising Video," whose campy irony was lost on her queer professor who after watching it blankly asked, "Is this a joke?" It was within this atmosphere of community building and general debauchery that I came out of the closet and discovered my love of all things queer, including *Stone Butch Blues.* Feinberg's book, like most queer fiction I read during this time, was passed around our group of friends from reader to reader, discussed at length and even read aloud, creating a sort of cult like craze. By the time I took up the book as the subject of my Master's thesis, it had been read by nearly everyone I know.

After discovering Delany, I realized that I could revive my previous work on Feinberg by applying Delany's theories of contact toward a reexamination of policing and agency within Feinberg's text. My initial reading, which now seems quite stale, focused on the ways in which police brutality hinders the expression of queer gender identities and sexual activities in public spaces like bathrooms and bars. While it is easy to read the gruesome scenes of police brutality in Feinberg's text as an example of the dichotomous existence between queer community building and the wrath of the police, Delany's model allows for a broader conception of policing and in turn, resistance to institutional controls. As a contact zone, the lesbian bars Feinberg depicts are characterized by sexual activity and interclass relationships, as well as by the self-policing that precedes and actually resists intervention by the police. When, for example, fifteen year old Jess is admitted into the bar without regard to her age, Jess quickly learns that queer bars have their own protocols and regulations, set in place largely to resist the police presence "pushing against our space" (29). Jess acknowledges the "rite of passage" (34) of adapting to the bar's unwritten rules—how to properly order drinks, befriend the butches, and dance with the femmes—an important induction into both adulthood and into the community. Delany, similarly, observes that picking up on and adapting to the self-governing rules of the porn theaters allows new young patrons to gain membership within this society. These rules, most importantly, are set in place not only to ensure comradery between members, but to counter the power of actual police officials. Butch/femme dress codes, Lillian Faderman observes, provided another instance of this self-policing, as regular patrons could easily identify nonconforming dressers as undercover cops (165). Internal control over this transgressive space allows patrons to prepare against raids by the police. For instance, when the police arrive at Feinberg's bar, the underage Jess is hidden away in a lavatory stall: "the cops were here. So there I crouched. For a long time. It wasn't until I frightened a femme half to death when she opened the stall door that I discovered the police had left long ago [. . .] no one remembered that the kid was hidden in the bathroom" (28). By forcing Jess out of the mainspace of the bar, the community can include younger members without facing legal repercussions by the police.

These democratic regulations, moreover, are determined by the architectural construction of queer spaces themselves. Delany, accordingly, depicts the layout of several porn theaters, illustrating that while a sense of propriety characterizes the outer realms visible from the street, the dark orchestra and horseshoe balconies become sexual free zones. Delany also describes the utility of having the theatres situated together in Times Square "where there were so many other kinds of activity around" (106) allowing gay men to remain "safe" (106) within this high traffic area. In *Stonewall: The Riots that Sparked the Revolution,* David Carter similarly illustrates the connections between the actual location of the Stonewall Inn, and its success as a site of resistance. The riots were possible, argues Carter, because of the urban planning surrounding the bar. "This tangle of irregular streets and triangular open spaces" (13) facilitated a blockade preventing police retaliation to the queer takeover of the bar, "using the Village's many side streets to circumvent the police tactics for clearing the streets" (191). These spatially facilitated riots, hailed as the birth of the gay rights movement, are a watershed moment in both queer history and in Feinberg's own life and work. To ascertain the significance of the Stonewall riots to Feinberg's texts, one need only open the front cover of any autographed edition to expose that first blank page bearing the inspiring trace of Feinberg's authorial presence: "To Rookie in the spirit of Stonewall . . ." This friend and I joked about how she was so excited that Feinberg had written her such an empowering personal message, only to discover that this was the motto etched on the opening pages of countless other friends' books. "The spirit of Stonewall," we concluded, was not a sign of Feinberg's personal recognition of any one of our secret powers to continue the fight for queer liberation, but rather an extension of the anti-authoritarianism and grassroots resistance that keep us reading Feinberg.

This community driven resistance to the police that remains so central to Feinberg is also an important tenant of Delany's theory of contact. Contact, Delany reveals, can take place between those without state power and those in positions of governing authority: "it can be the conversation that starts with any service persons—mailman, policeman, librarian, store clerk or counter person" (123). Contact thus opens up a discursive space within which authority can be negotiated and shared. Policing, as both Feinberg and Delany suggest, need not be a one-sided, uncontested event, but can rather emerge as a result of dialogue in which citizens choose and enforce self-regulation over the violent controls of the state. Deviant behavior can instead be kept in check by citizens themselves through nonviolent means. Through imagined as notoriously violent places, cities, Delany reveals, actually "keep their violence rate monumentally lower than in small towns by the self-policing practices that come from 'eyes on the street,' *supported by a rich system of relatively random benefits and rewards that encourage pleasant sociality based largely on contact*" (156). Delany elaborates that self-policing is made possible not merely because of the "*number* of eyes on the street" (154) but because those who inhabit the cityscape have a particular "investment" (154) in the relations exhibited within their communities. Delany warns us that forces of development and gentrification, as well as poverty and economic stratification can negate this process: "too high a proportion of strangers to indigenes, too high a turnover of regular population, and the process breaks down [. . .] produc[ing] the dangerous neighborhoods: the housing project, the park with not enough stores and eating spaces bordering on it, the blocks and blocks of apartment residences without any ameliorating human services" (154). In such neighborhoods, safety, surveillance, and control are left in the hands of the police, whom often serve as the source of violence rather than a tool for its prevention.

This observation comes without surprise, as much literature has already addressed the proliferation of police brutality in urban centers like New York. Coming to popularity with their republications in the 1970s, books like *A Brief Treatise on The Police of the City of New York* marked a revival of nineteenth century estimations of the importance of state policing "to guard," "to prevent," and "to punish" (4), marking a renewed interest in the function and abuse of state sanctioned controls within the metropolis. James Richardson's *The New York Police: Colonial Times to 1901*, also published in 1970, traces the inception and development of the New York City police force, illustrating that political corruption has always been the central impetus behind police employment, and that "police brutality and abuse of authority flourished in such a climate of distrust" (287). More recent accounts of police violence are addressed in volumes like Sheila

Fitzgerald's *Police Brutality*, a college textbook-like examination of factors including race and corruption that motivate police, and Skolnick and Fyfe's, *Above the Law: Police and the Excessive Use of Force*, a response to the Rodney King beating that advocates "openness about police and what they do" (266). These two volumes both suggest that police brutality can be attributed in part to a lack of accountability and community involvement within economically stratified areas, pointing back to Delany's recommendation for neighborhood diversity and self-policing. Other studies like Frank Donner's *Protectors of Privilege: Red Squads and Police Repression in Urban America*, characterize policing as "the protective arm of the economic and political interests of the capitalist system" (1) reiterating Richardson's earlier connection between police brutality and the maintenance of the status quo, a thesis familiarized by Michel Foucault's seminal *Discipline and Punish*, which traces violent policing strategies back to earlier practices of public torture predating the prison system.

More recent literature also provides insight into the effects of 9-11 upon incidents of violence by the police. In "Trickle-Down Terror: The Effect of Post 9-11 Politics on Queer Youth of Color in NYC," Kenyon Farrow addresses the ways in which "white institutions support individual acts of violence against queer youth of color specifically [. . .] with acts of physical violence or institutional oppression" (11). Farrow acknowledges that "heavy policing is something that oppressed communities have had to live with in New York City for many years under the Quality of Life Initiative [. . .] a strategic effort by the NYPD to aggressively ticket and prosecute people for committing petty offenses like public urination, loitering or solicitation" (11). Farrow also reveals that "since 9-11 . . . police presence has steadily increased" (11). Farrow traces this onslaught of police brutality back to the Stonewall era in which Feinberg's narrative is set. He illustrates how gentrification measures "left queer youth of color with no access to public space they had long ago claimed" (12). Farrow also reminds us that "being militarized and policed is nothing new. If you are a queer youth of color in New York City who hangs out in the West Village, you are being policed by the Sixth Precinct (which added 23 rookie cops to its precinct in February 2002), the NY/NJ Port Authority, the NYPD Narcotics Unit, New York State Parks Patrol, as well as several community policing operatives, including the Christopher Street Patrol and Residents In Distress (also known as RID)" (12). Unlike the volumes discussed above that see community policing as a solution to violence, Farrow highlights the complicity of community policing efforts with the racist institutions of the police. He exposes how gentrification and development motivate communities to police residents of color as part of their mandate to push them out of the neighborhood. Community policing, then, stands in opposition to Delany's conception of self-policing, which diverts authority away from a centralized power in the hopes of cultivating rather than eliminating class and racial difference.

Times Square Red, Times Square Blue, accordingly, grapples with this tenuous but important distinction between self-policing toward the goal of diversity, and community policing established to reconfigure a neighborhood from a place of interracial, interclass contact to one of sterilized middle class, segregationism. While Delany depicts Times Square to exemplify the detrimental effects of "the economic 'redevelopment' of a highly diversified neighborhood with working-class residences and small human services" (148) into "a predominantly middle-class area" (160), one need not look far in New York to discover a plethora of instances of legally enforced gentrification. Visiting the West Village, home of the Stonewall Inn, provides one example of a community once saturated in police violence that now exhibits the wealthy, assimilationist gays and young urban heterosexuals who have sterilized the streets with their doggie gyms and upscale maternity stores, erasing traces of what was once remembered by Carter as a transgressive, interclass, racially diverse enclave for queers. *Stone Butch Blues* illustrates exactly this process, as the policing of gay bars that occurs throughout the text is intended to thwart the interclass and interracial bonding, sexual and otherwise, that Jess seeks out in the novel. When Jess is violently apprehended by the police, beaten, and then kicked in the ribs "for punctuation" (57), Jess is labeled a "fuckin' traitor" (57), calling attention to not only Jess's sexual transgressions as a "bulldagger" (56) but also to the alliance formed between the white Jess and Ed, who is black. Although Jess and Ed speak out against the racism that pervades their own community, they cannot win the battle against the police who represent the urge to keep "segregation alive and well" (55). As Delany reminds us, "any social form (or, indeed, architectural form) that shies us away from contact and contact-like situations [. . .] is likely to be approved" (164). The role of the police, consequently, is to prevent contact and to restructure neighborhoods from self-policing communities to segregated enclaves characterized by lack of diversity, institutional violence, and perpetual fear.

Living in Brooklyn, it becomes nearly impossible not to witness this violence firsthand, as the immense police presence distributed unevenly throughout the borough marks the astounding rate at which many neighborhoods are becoming irreparably gentrified, a process in which as a young, white, middle-class student, I feel unavoidably complicit. On the first warm Friday night of spring, when most of Brooklyn's residents had poured out onto the street to enjoy the good weather, my friends and I were evacuated off of the 'R' train at 36th Street, a way station between the notoriously gentrified Park Slope and Sunset Park, a predominantly working-class, Latin neighborhood and home of my first New York apartment. While the neighborhood did not yet resemble the yuppified Park

Slope, my own building was already overwhelmed by young, mostly white hipsters and queers like myself who were priced out of trendier areas, and my friends' block (where my landlords also resided) was also nicknamed "Vanilla Lane." Upon leaving the terminally delayed subway car at 36th Street to walk the twenty blocks home, we entered a train platform riddled with fully armed policemen, while NYPD helicopters flew overhead, beaming searchlights across the outdoor tracks. Deciding that it would be wiser to walk along the commercial Fifth Avenue instead of along the police infested subway route, my friends and I watched as squad cars stopped at each block to handcuff and arrest a nonthreatening looking civilian on every single corner of every block. The events of this evening sent a clear message about the changing of the guard that was about to take place in community membership and local authority, a change already signaled by NYPD security cameras on lampposts and the "Economic Development" truck that removes graffiti from storefront grates. Self-policing was no longer an option once the neighborhood was literally invaded by both plainclothes and uniformed police threatening to dissuade contact and to restructure the diverse institutions and demographics that made Sunset Park a lively and safe place to live.

Delany also addresses the displacement that results from gentrification and redevelopment, observing that "what has happened to Times Square has already made my life, personally, somewhat more lonely and isolated. I have talked with a dozen men whose sexual outlets, like many of mine, were centered on that neighborhood. It is the same for them. We need contact" (175). Delany laments the loss of the old Times Square, emphasizing the importance of spaces that accommodate "needs that most of our society does not yet know how to acknowledge" (90). Delany mirrors Jess's own quest for an outlet through which to enact a queer sexual identity, of finding "the place I could fit" (27). Just as *Stone Butch Blues* illustrates the susceptibility to violence that the butches undergo while patronizing their designated spaces, Delany reveals that relocating queer spaces from Times Square to the waterfront will expose their patrons to "muggers, bashers, not to mention all the legal forms of exploitation [. . .] the police can still nail anyone and any place they want to. That means, when they want to, they will!" (106) Negotiating both a massive police presence and the dissolution of spaces elemental to queer existence, it becomes difficult to challenge authority "in the spirit of Stonewall" when faced with the corporatism, classism, racism, and xenophobia that has since splintered and commercialized the movement.

Living in New York and feeling at a loss for Delany's queer contact, it becomes difficult to imagine oneself successfully fighting back against those who have already obliterated so much of our space. But rather than conclude pessimistically, I would like to recall *Times Square,* the 1980 film by Allan Moyle that takes up so many of Delany's concerns. *Times Square* depicts the coming of age of two girls who form an interclass relationship that empowers them to quite effectively speak out against politicians and developers in order to preserve the area, all the while evading capture by the police. In the director's commentary on the DVD, Moyle expresses his relief that the film was even made, simply for its having captured what the area used to be like before it became "like Disneyland." Moyle also reveals that while the relationship between the two heroines was supposed to be explicitly lesbian, the producer cut all of the sexual scenes between them. The film, as a result, actually normalizes itself in much the same spirit that Times Square has been liquefied since. Viewers, however, remain free to embrace the queerness still suggested throughout the film. I personally know many people who regard *Times Square* as a model for continued resistance, as I have seen the faces of the young lovers on flyers and posters advertising queer events. Contact, the film still shows, is in fact possible, and self-policing can overpower what initially appears an incontestable force.

These opportunities for queer resistance are exactly what Feinberg celebrates as "the sprit of Stonewall." In his account of the Stonewall riots, Carter points to the importance of such creative strategies of resistance to the police. He documents that while "getting a busted head" (193), or dodging "swinging nightsticks" (193), protesters cleverly managed to retort with cries like, we "should catch the police, rip their clothes off, and screw them on the spot" (193). He recalls another group of street youth who formed a "Rockette kick line" (177), confronting a fully armed policeman while chanting, "we're the Village girls, we wear our hair in curls, we wear our dungarees above our nelly knees, and with the constables, we simply hypnotize" (177). Aware of how such events frame an ongoing history of queer resistance to the police, Feinberg's text celebrates the capacity of queer communities to subvert state sanctioned authorities in the face of classism, racism, and gender-based oppression. Reading Feinberg in tandem with Delany allows us to rethink and resist institutional controls in their various guises. Aspiring to achieve neighborhood diversity and interclass contact will require a massive rethinking of the ways in which capitalism overdetermines our physical surroundings and, as Delany reminds us, we must challenge the economic status quo before our cityscapes can improve.

BIBLIOGRAPHY

Carter, David. *Stonewall: The Riots that Sparked the Gay Revolution*. New York: St. Martin's, 2004.

Christian, Charles. *A Brief Treatise on the Police of the City of New York*. New York: Arno, 1970.

Delany, Samuel R. *Times Square Red, Times Square Blue.* New York: New York UP, 1999.

Donner, Frank. *Protectors of Privilege: Red Squads and Police Repression in Urban America.* Berkeley: California UP, 1990.

Faderman, Lillian. *Odd Girls and Twilight Lovers: A History of Lesbian Life in 20th Century America.* New York: Columbia UP, 1991.

Farrow, Kenyon. "Trickle-Down Terror: The Effect of Post 9-11 Politics on Queer Youth of Color in NYC." *Objector* (Summer 2003): 11

Feinberg, Leslie. *Stone Butch Blues*. Los Angeles: Alyson, 2003.

Fitzgerald, Sheila. Ed. *Police Brutality*. Detroit: Thompson, 2007.

Foucault, Michel. *Discipline and Punish.* Trans. Alan Sheridan. New York: Vintage, 1977.

Moyle, Allan, director. *Times Square* (film). 1980.

Pratt, Mary Louise. "Arts of the Contact Zone." *Profession* (1991): 33–40.

Richardson, James F. *The New York Police: Colonial Times to 1901.* New York: Oxford UP, 1970.

Shakur, Assata. *Assata: An Autobiography*. Chicago: Zed, 1987.

Skolnick, Jerome H. and Fyfe, James J. *Above the Law: Police and Excessive Use of Force.* New York: Macmillan, 1993.

6

Read at Your Own Risk

Jennifer Mitchell

YOU ARE WHAT YOU READ

I am painfully proud of my bookshelves. Some quaint, though perhaps trite manifestation of a Victorian domestic ideal, I always used to envision living in a dark house with bookshelves lining all the walls. That huge house is a charming three-bedroom apartment in Brooklyn, New York, and those walls of shelved books are simply three separate mismatched bookcases. The first one, in the living room, alphabetically chronicles A through O. The second, near our attempt at a "study," contains O through Z—and some other haphazard texts that fit nowhere (think St. Martin's Handbook or a course packet on Feminism). The last, however, is what greets visitors, standing tall in the foyer. The twinges of anal-retentiveness that compel me to make my bed every morning have expressed themselves not in alphabetical organization, but rather, in a thematic division of shelf space. It is filled with the texts that will be a part of my dissertation—the texts that have dictated and will dictate my future as a scholar, and perhaps as a person.

This is the bookcase that matters.

After I first moved in, a friend of a friend popped over for dinner, took a gander at these books and asked, in a completely non-ironic way, if I like Stephen King. Of course, after I laughed and mentioned my negligible middle-school exposure to Mr. King, I realized that Keith simply did not know how to read the me that the collection of texts implied. This funny and sweet interaction inspired Erin, my roommate, to pose the following life-altering question (life-altering for me, anyway): "Can you even imagine what people must think of you if they only see these books?"

No. I can't. Awkward, nervous giggle.

But, when I actually sat down to think about it, I tried to. I looked from title to title, at texts arranged by author, by subject, by whether they are fiction, anthologies, theoretical texts, etc. and I attempted to read my self vis-à-vis my library. Erin posed the question about the relationship between my self and my texts because of the books on these shelves. Take your pick from a sample of them: *Faggots* by Larry Kramer, *Epistemology of the Closet* by Eve Sedgwick, *Women as Lovers* by Elfriede Jelinek, *The Invention of Pornography* by Lynn Hunt, *Roxana* by Daniel Defoe, *Male Fantasies* (both volumes) by Klaus Theweleit, *The Apparitional Lesbian* by Terry Castle, *The 120 Days of Sodom* by Marquis de Sade, *A Mind of Its Own: A Cultural History of the Penis* by David Friedman, *Hogg* by Samuel Delaney, *Fantomina, or Love in a Maze* by Eliza Haywood. (The afterthought of Erin's question, was, of course, whether I was a gay man or a lesbian, but the mention of only those two possible sexual beings seems to warrant its own discussion. Moreover, would it be possible for me to have a self that exists within these bookshelves—within these texts—that may or may not be the same as the self that hops on the subway, pays her rent, and cooks big pots of soup? I hope so.) This bookcase contains texts that span the last three hundred years. They are written by authors—male, female, trans/hetero, homo, bi. They are about any number of the following subjects: sex, gender, identity, masochism, sadism, love, lust, passion, books, people, history, war, intellectuals, dreams, reality, the past, the present, the future.

The spectrum that is created by the grouping of these texts is precisely what Erin was getting at when she asked about the connections between these books, the I who reads them, and the perceptions of others attempting to read us both. In "Unpacking My Library: A Talk about Book Collecting," Walter Benjamin attempts to give us "some insight into the relationship of a book collector to his possessions, into collecting rather than a collection"(60). I am not a book collector according to Benjamin's vision, concerned with "dates, place names, formats, previous owners, bindings, and the like"(63). (Though, of course, I am always curious to see the markings in the margins made by hands that possessed these books before I did. I was particularly amused by a giant "WTF?" on page 61 in my used copy of David Halperin's *How to do the History of Homosexuality.* Moreover, I enjoyed the thoroughly eerie experience of recently having reread my own copy of George Gissing's *The Odd Women* and saying "ugh" aloud upon Everard's marriage, only to then look further down the page at my own handwriting having written "ugh" in purple pen nearly a decade ago.) Yet, Benjamin invites his readers, at the beginning of this essay, to join him amidst the stacks of his books, to ponder the nature of collecting and the act of acquisition. My library—the books that have deliberately been brought together because of my interests—is just as much the subject of this chapter as is its writer. This literary experiment, the direct result of Erin's prompt, is a different kind of unpacking: an exploration of the relationship between my body of texts and the (often implicit) construction of my academic and personal identity. What follows is strange and quirky. At least ideally.

In many ways, it could also be a mess. But, as I read, I am being read. From strangers in the subway who give funny looks based upon the covers that they see from across a car (think the boldly titled *Homos* or the erotically charged image on the cover of *Faggots*) to the most intimate of friends who are still surprised by the things that I say or do, the act of reading elicits being read. The readings of texts that follow—of rather infuriating work by Kathy Acker, of "traditional" Victorian literature by Charlotte Brontë, and of what I'd consider the "genre" of masochistic texts—are readings that prompt me to configure and reconfigure my sense of self, both scholarly and otherwise. The bookshelf, my library, tells my fortune. It invites missteps, mistakes, and misinterpretation. Just as my reading of the texts on it falls into the same set of traps.

A IS FOR ILLEGIBILITY

I start, predictably, at the beginning—or at some semblance of a beginning: the letter "A," for Acker.

In "A Few Notes on Two of My Books," Kathy Acker writes: "I've never been sure about the need for literary criticism. If a work is immediate enough, alive enough, the proper response isn't to be academic, to write about it, but to use it, to go on. By using each other, each other's texts, we keep on living, imagining, making, fucking, and we fight this society to death"(7). Acker's fundamental belief in plagiarism is, in my mind, what distinguishes her from other avant-garde-esque punk-rock-writers. The acknowledgment that one is constantly revisiting, reclaiming and reusing texts already written drastically altered my conception of what it means to write, to be a writer.

Perhaps more importantly, however, my engagement with Acker and a number of her texts drastically altered my conception of what it meant to read, to be a reader.

Amidst a "narrative" that details an incestuous relationship, a linguistic conquest, and a redefinition of Nathaniel Hawthorne's *The Scarlet Letter*, the dream maps are critical and literal interruptions in *Blood and Guts in High School*. They start—if start is the apt word—with a hopeful declaration: "I learn to fly" which is followed by a series of arrows and narrative commentary—

> turn in circles, barely . . . I get to like flying . . . a big bird starts to chase me . . . a black bird . . . it gets closer and closer . . . I have to learn to fly better . . . it's still

> getting closer . . . as soon as it catches me, I'll have to die . . . I have to fly across the whole world . . . T H ~~E~~ W ~~O~~ R L ~~D~~ . . . but the bird keeps following me no mater how well I fly . . . I have nowhere else to go. I go back. (46–47)

My eye follows the arrow, reading the words, attempting to impose a logical critical text upon it. Attempt #1: Flying is writing,[1] the big black bird is patriarchy—whether manifest in bodies or in language—the strikethroughs on "T H E W O R L D" speak to the desire to write on the bird, marking the bird as fair game; there is a final, possibly defeated retreat to a sort of universal starting point. Going back, though, implies going forward as the arrows correspond with another narrative track: "The bird's almost on top of me . . . closer . . . ZOOM . . . closer . . . I don't care what happens. I'm so tired, I give up. I decide to let the bird catch me. I fall, the huge black bird catches me and folds me in his arms. As soon as I give up to him, he falls in love with me. We try to figure out how to save me from death. THE END OF THE WORLD" (47). This text and the arrows correspond to probably only 10 percent of the first dream map. The arrows are what prompt the reader to look for any direction, as his/her engagement would otherwise be overshadowed by the large vaginal image of "Black Water" or the oddly shaped penis image of "the city." Nonetheless, the arrows and the corresponding snippets of text tell a story. A story that is difficult, if not impossible to decipher—at least with the decoding tools that we are taught or given. The bird—my instinctive reading of language—falls in love with the speaker who is trying so desperately to transcend the limitations of its chase and its presumed power. The possibility of violence and conquest is countered by a rather romantic description of enclosure and safety—of protectively being surrounded.

The first dream map in the sequence is a labyrinth with no marked path. You follow one, and hit a wall. You start over, follow another, and find yourself stuck in a Greek temple with no way out. By declaring them dreams, Acker puts the reader into conversation with Freud; yet it is a conversation that is, ultimately, fruitless. Our desire to interpret and to make sense of what appears in front of us is met with brutal prohibitions. Even invoking a theory of the unconscious gets us literally nowhere. While inviting us to try to cohere what appears on the pages, Acker is simultaneously forbidding the employment of any overarching cohesive logic.

She asks the question in "A Few Notes," "Does 'make' mean 'create'?" (9) and she plays with the answer to that question with the copyright that appears in the bottom right-hand corner of the page "from *BLOOD AND GUTS IN HIGH SCHOOL* c. Kathy Acker, 1977" (47). Acker's self-reflexivity is funny. And frustrating. Whether or not Acker has made or created anything is almost beside the point. What we, as readers—what I, as reader—make or create out of it, is something else entirely. Today, the dream maps are my bookshelves—an apparent unit on display that virtually begs for the imposition of coherence. (The bookshelves in particular warrant their own narrative: a slightly tarnished "reject" from the IKEA As-Is section; stackable black handpainted shelves that my father built; and a bulky plastic unit that travelled with me from St. Louis to New York. Origins that are a vital part of my own personal fable.) The narrative of the self ascribed to the "I" of the dream maps is parallel to the narrative of the self ascribed to the "I" of my library. Yet, Acker's dream maps refuse the imposition. They fight me and my critical eye (I) for the duration of my readerly engagement with them. And that is, of course, the point. The act of reading, for Acker, and of Acker's texts, is struggle and entanglement, while the act of writing is piracy.

Unpacking my library vis-à-vis Kathy Acker might mean that I am illegible because I want to be and because I have to be.

Or, it might mean that I create myself—and am myself created—from what has come before me.

B IS FOR FAIRY TALES

In English literature graduate departments, much like high school, there are types. There are the Joyce-obsessed, dick-waving men and the painfully self-involved emotive poets, who can, thankfully, be male, female, or anything in between and beyond. (I know that this list will undoubtedly yield scoffs and dismissive eye-rolls, yet I stand by its validity, unfortunate or not.) Without fail, however, there are the Jane-Austen-Is-A-Goddess-girls. We all know them. They think in terms of Mr. Darcy, sigh at particularly cheesy moments in novels, movies, even classroom discussions. Often, they have this slightly dreamy, slightly distant, slightly crazy look in their eyes, perhaps a testament to their unfortunate placement in this particular century. To be honest, Jane Austen has her rightful place on my bookshelf, surrounded by the weighty Victorian novels about family, class, loss, love, regret, religion, manners, and propriety.

These are often books about love. Big, huge, life-changing, life-making love.

In *Sexual Politics*, Kate Millett writes of the sexual revolution inherent in Charlotte Brontë's *Villette* that

> Lucy is free. Free is alone; given a choice between "love" in its most agreeable contemporary manifestation, and freedom, Lucy chose to retain the individualist humanity she had shored up, even at the expense of sexuality. The sentimental reader is also free to call Lucy "warped," but Charlotte Brontë is hard-minded enough to know that there was no man in Lucy's society with whom she could have lived and still been free. (146)

Millett, who finds Lucy both compelling and frustrating, is interested in Brontë's insistence that marriage is a rather doomed institution for complicated women. To be fair, of course, the novel ends with Lucy's declaration of her love: "M. Emanuel was away three years. Reader, they were the three happiest years of my life" (461). M. Emanuel/M. Paul, Lucy's love—though perhaps Millett would characterize him otherwise—leaves for a colonially based economic project immediately after his declaration of love and his presentation of his gift of a school to and for her. His absence, in which Lucy works so that the school, and she, will flourish, is what she speaks of in this passage. She realizes the strange implications of such a statement: "Do you scout that paradox?" (461). The paradox is located within the perceived relation between the closeness of one's beloved and consequential happiness; without one, the presumption exists that the other is impossible. Lucy explains the happiness of those three years as the direct result of her work and her independence—all superficially convincing reasons, of course. Yet, the spectrum of happiness is colored by the tragic insinuation at the end of the novel: that M. Paul may have perished in a storm heading back to Lucy. The ambiguity of the ending of the novel suggests that the two possibilities that face Lucy at the end of those three years—a marriage to M. Paul upon his return or mourning him upon his passing—are equally devastating. While Millett celebrates Lucy's freedom, her escape from domestic devastation, my students are heartbroken. They are devastated because they wanted Lucy with her equal, M. Paul, to triumph over Polly and John, Ginevra and the Count—the novel's other representations of "love."

Yet, they don't realize that she does.

The Lucy Snowe that I read in *Villette* is happy because of a realization of her own sexual potential. The sturdy, plain, suffering girl that Lucy presents herself as is only half-true—if that. The erotically charged, antagonistic, intense girl that M. Paul brings out is the half that lies beneath the surface. The half that, once we realize she exists, we can identify in Lucy all throughout. It is with the knowledge of sexual selfhood that Lucy is able to take charge of her own school, her own life, and her own future. Lucy, having finally been objectified by someone worthy of the challenge, is fundamentally able to objectify herself. The presumption that Lucy, having awoken into sexual desire and desirability, would allow her sexuality to shrivel upon the absence of her presumed partner is absurd. The fear or belief that Lucy never consummates her relationship is tragic; rather, the relationship that warrants sexual consummation is the one that Lucy has with herself. The three "happiest" years for our narrator are masturbatory. And satisfyingly so.

Villette is not *Pride and Prejudice*. Thankfully—both for me, and for Lucy.

Unpacking my library vis-à-vis Brontë might mean that I believe epic love to be tragic love. The bigger they are, the harder they fall?

Or it might mean that my hopeless romanticism manifests itself in the powerful possibilities opened up by autoeroticism.

C IS FOR MY NAUGHTY DRAWER

There is, unquestionably, a set of standard "getting to know you" questions when you meet someone new. The most pressing and obvious:

> What do you do? I teach and I'm in grad school.
> What do you teach? I teach literature and composition to college students.
> What are you in school for? English literature.
> What's your specialty? That's sort of hard to explain.
> How so? Well, I write about masochism.
> Insert inquisitive look.

The array of responses is varied: there is always a momentary silence and an effort to regain composure, a confused yet piqued interest in books, and an implicit or explicit gesture toward my personal life. An arched eyebrow, a wink, a knowing glance—each physical reaction is an act of reading. Yet, the third shelf on the bookcase, filled with books like *Masochism in Modern Man, Story of O, Coldness and Cruelty, Venus in Furs,* begs a host of more elaborate questions about my sense of self, and sexuality—about what is presumed to be hidden in my naughty drawer and how that is manifest in my scholarship.

Katherine Davis begins her introduction to *Coming to Power,* a text about "S/M lesbians" by writing that "This is an outrageous book" (7). The claim to outrageousness is a testament to audience. While readers may have previous experience with scholarly essays, personal interviews, erotica and pornographic materials, their conglomerative force within this text all underneath the content-based umbrella of graphic sadomasochism is presumed to be innovative and pioneering: "*Coming to Power* is a statement, a confrontation, and a challenge" (12). The editors of this collection conceive of themselves as actively working against a set of problematic notions about the reality of sadomasochism. Yet, the subject of S/M pops up in all sorts of scholarly places. From Leo Bersani's *Homos* to Kate Millett's *Sexual Politics,* academia has fostered an interest in the way what we may (or may not do) in the bedroom—far beyond the heter-homo binary that underscores queer theory—could and, presumably, does inflect the way that we read texts and the insights we can pull from them.

Thanks to the observations of even the earliest sexologists, masochism as a deliberate sexual perversion was considered to plague only men for a very specific reason. Havelock Ellis writes that "masochism is more especially found in men; this may be in part be because in women a certain degree of sexual subjection, the primary stage of masochism, may fairly be regarded as almost normal" (207). Sexual subjugation is not only a "normal" experience for women, it is part and parcel of being a woman. Freudian psychoanalysis suggests that female passivity, an ideal and inherent part of femininity, is itself masochistic. Women—at least the good ones—relish their subjected position, being on the receiving end of the always active, always male pursuit of sex. Marie Bonaparte writes that "In coitus, the woman, in effect, is subjected to a sort of beating by the man's penis. She receives its blows and often, even, loves their violence" (87). With the equation of violence and intercourse in mind, the editors of *Coming to Power* find themselves in interesting territory. Of course, there is no penis with which to be beaten, yet they are fighting the pervasive belief about the inherent masochistic character of women, attempting to reveal S/M as an empowering sexual possibility rather than an intrinsic part of feminine weakness.

But even the mention of masochism conjures up false—and also, though less often, true representations of sexual and personal identities. Take, for instance, the title of Anita Phillips's examination *A Defense of Masochism*. Early on in her introduction, Phillips wants to make clear that her project is, in many ways, a redemption of a misunderstood sexual choice: "By bringing masochism into focus I hope to prevent it being used as a kind of emotional and sexual waste-basket, a receptacle for the odds and ends of people's behaviour, for the things they cannot explain about themselves but still feel strongly" (4). Phillips, although she frames her analysis of masochism within the confines of her content heterosexual relationship, finds herself obeying the same impulse as Davis: that masochism warrants a defense.

Yet, masochism was, once upon a time, its own defense. (And, notably, its own offense.) Marguerite Porete, a Beguine mystic, writes in *The Mirror of Simple Souls* of her relationship with God in terms that are so intensely erotic and so powerfully masochistic, that it is almost no wonder that she was convicted of heresy and executed in 1310. Porete devoutly craves abjection; she becomes more and more obsessed with the possibility of being negated by an all-powerful God. What starts out as a fairly traditional treatise on the meaning of virtue and sinlessness and devotion to God evolves into an eroticized doctrine of abuse. That abuse, however, is subsumed by her belief in *love*: "She does not care about herself. She cares about God, who loves her more than this Soul could love herself" (89). God's love is initially—and rightfully, according to her contemporaries—wholly sustaining in its grace; yet it is not grace that Porete continuously wants, but rather all-encompassing passion: "Thus such a Soul, says Love, is so enflamed in the furnace of the first of love that she has become properly fire" (107).[2] The furnace of love that appears throughout the text allows Porete the metaphorical space in which to lust after God.

This lust is not simply one-dimensional, but rather it becomes dialogic as Porete enables God to respond to her desires. Porete, by virtue of her position as speaker, coerces the character of God into a specified authority. She begs for an interactive relationship that necessitates suffering *and* pleasure, more aptly, pleasure through suffering. "*And then again I said to Him that if it were possible that He could give me as great torments as He is great in power to avenge Himself of me and of my sins, if it would please Him, it would be pleasing to me*" (212; author's emphasis). Porete highlights several things in this particular passage:

Her position in one-to-one contact with God.
Her desire for what he *could* give her.
Her ability to influence his desire to give it.
Her need to be purged or sin.
Her need to be punished.
The pleasure that she would receive if he would infinitely torment her.

Medieval mystics are often looking for a way to align themselves with the suffering of Christ; the gory focus of many devotional texts leads the reader onto the crucifix and into the wounds of Christ himself (See, for instance, *The Writings of Richard Rolle*). Though perhaps seeming blasphemous, it follows a wholly logical trajectory. In *Masochism and Modern Man*, Theodor Reik writes of the connection between specific religious figures, experiences and sexual masochism: "Christ's very life and death became the glorification of suffering and its conquest. The royal way of the cross becomes the path that all mankind should walk" (347). The appropriation of Christ as exemplar is manifest in these early mystical texts.

Yet, what Porete is doing here seems quite different than an associative empathy through imaginative identification. Instead, her request is actually a test for God—a God that is, in many ways, detached from the bodily figure of Christ. Just how much can he torment a person? Just how powerful is he? Within Porete's desire to be subject, to be dominated, to suffer is the desire to see what is within the realm of torturous possibilities. She is, literally, "asking for it" by asking for what could be done that is worse than all that has been done before and all that could be done in the future.

What she is explicitly asking for, though, is not a good spanking or even a satisfying display of humiliation but utter annihilation. She wants to be negated into nothingness; she presumes that such an act will yield pleasure for both God and herself. The love that she initially bases this treatise on—represented by terms like "Justice" and "Mercy"—has evolved into such an extreme that Porete is panting with anticipation. While Reik suggests that "scientists" have consistently misread the relationship between martyrdom and sexual masochism, Porete's ultimate desire is to be made erotically extinct directly by an active, sexual God.

Convicted of heresy for the second time, Porete is burned alive. The will of God that has inspired and guided her to write this book has conspired with those who find it and her dangerous, and in need of punishment. The sentence is carried through. Porete becomes the fire that has built in her heart. She is, thus, negated—a final, everlasting orgasm. That orgasm is intrinsically tied to self-awareness and enlightenment; Porete's selfhood is only actualized the moment that it is entirely denied. As O, Pauline Reage's masochistic protoype is told, "Your one and only duty: to lend yourself. Your hands are not your own, nor are your breasts, nor, most especially any of your bodily orifices, which we may explore or penetrate at will . . . this is less for our pleasure than for your enlightenment" (15-17). Masochism is both the means and the end.

Anita Phillips feels compelled to defend masochism by suggesting that its "final, unexpected message is to forget yourself" (164). She relies upon the story inherent in masochistic fantasies as the defining element of masochism and one that, if agreed upon, is simply an interest in narrative possibility. Yet, Phillips's stance about the core of masochistic play does not go uncontested. In "Courtly Love, or Woman as Thing," Slavoj Zizek writes "Masochism confronts us with the paradox of the symbolic order *qua* the order of 'fictions': there is more truth in the mask we wear, in the game we play, in the 'fiction' we obey and follow, than in what is concealed beneath the mask. The very kernel of the masochist's being is externalized in the staged game towards which he maintains his constant distance" (92). For his reading of masochism, heavily influenced by Lacan's own analysis of courtly love (see "Courtly Love as Anamorphosis"), masochistic engagement reveals the core, the "kernel" of oneself. Instead of forgetting the self, according to Zizek, masochism allows for the unraveling of its previously bound existence. The conversation that could take place between Phillips and Zizek is a conversation about truth and being, about the way we live, engage with others, get our kicks, and figure out who we are—either by disavowal or by affirmation—or by a dreamy combination of the two.

Unpacking my library vis-à-vis masochism might mean that my work is fantasy.

Or, it might mean, that fantasy is my work.

MY BODY (OF BOOKS)

When I published my first paper, my mother asked what it was about. In response, I said, "Do you know what the word 'cunt' means?" She, adorably and innocently (envision a rather hilarious scene when I explained crabs as more than seafood), said "No. What is it?" I told her to ask her youngest daughter. She and my father—and most other people with whom I come into contact—often wonder how I got involved in this stuff in a scholarly sense: porn, S/M, erotica, queer theory, gender studies, if it was at one point considered perverse, it has worked its way into the scope of my reading world. (I think as elements of my personal life, they would be significantly more understandable even to my parents.)

These bookshelves are a huge part of myself—the part that is interested in sexuality, that still, maybe too idealistically, thinks that there is innovative work to be done in that realm. The part of myself that realizes that my identity—both scholarly and otherwise—is constantly changing. New books, new ideas, new shapes, new abstractions, new directions. The spectrum of sexuality that sexologists like Richard von Krafft-Ebing began to conceive of, that behaviorists like Alfred Kinsey insisted upon, and that people all around the world live from day to day is read into and out of my texts, into and out of my life. My bookshelves not only represent where I've been but potentially where I will go. I see, like Benjamin, the moment of acquisition, when these books became mine.

When they became apart of the life that I lead as a reader. When they became a part of my literary body. These books are, in many ways, my body. Among scars and wounds, spankings, swaying hips, a wry smile, there are erogenous zones built into my library and me.

Your eye scans my bookshelves, pausing over texts that sound scandalous, that are scandalous, that I make scandalous, that you make into me. Read at your own risk.

NOTES

1. In her feminist text, *Woman and Nature: The Roaring Inside Her*, Susan Griffin writes "Desire is a force inside us. Our mouths drop open in the rushing air. Our bodies float among the stars. And we laugh in ecstasy to know the air has wishes; the stars want. 'Yes,' we call out, full of ourselves and delight. 'Yes,' we sing. 'We fly through the night'" (178). The treatise against patriarchy is ultimately filled with moments of break, like this one, in which flying is a metaphor for existence without constraint. Though Acker's plagiaristic politics imply constraint, flying can also be liberation to the extent that it is ever viable.

2. Porete's desire for fire—and the insinuation that she actually becomes fire as a result of the power of this passion—is satiated when, convicted of heresy for a second time, she is burned alive.

BIBLIOGRAPHY

Acker, Kathy. *Blood and Guts in High School.* New York: Grove, 1978.

——. *Bodies of Work.* New York: Serpent's Tail, 1997.

Benjamin, Walter. *Illuminations*. Trans. Harry Zohn. New York: Schocken Books, 1969.

Bonaparte, Marie. *Female Sexuality*. New York: Grove, 1965.

Brontë, Charlotte. *Villette*. New York: Signet Classics, 2004.

Ellis, Havelock. *Psychology of Sex: A Manual for Students*. New York: Emerson, 1938.

Griffin, Susan. *Woman and Nature: The Roaring Inside Her*. San Francisco: Sierra Club, 1978.

Millett, Kate. *Sexual Politics*. New York: Simon Schuster, 1970.

Phillips, Anita. *A Defense of Masochism*. New York: St. Martin's, 1998.

Porete, Marguerite. *The Mirror of Simple Souls*. Trans. Ellen L. Babinsky. New York: Paulist, 1993.

Reage, Pauline. *Story of O*. 1954. Trans. Sabine d'Estrée. New York: Grove, 1965.

Reik, Theodor. *Masochism in Modern Man*. Trans. Margaret H. Beigel and Gertrud M. Kurth. New York: Grove, 1941.

SAMOIS, eds. *Coming to Power: Writings and Graphics on Lesbian S/M*. 3rd Ed. Boston: Alyson, 1987.

Zizek, Slavoj. "Courtly Love, or, Woman as Thing." *The Metastases of Enjoyment: On Women and Causality*. London: Verso, 2005.

7

Realizations about Connections: A Literacy/Teaching Narrative

Nicholas Wright

The computer screen displays the following message, "You are not connected to the Internet." The Lucida Grande-Bold font, the twenty-five font size, and the gray font color at fifty percent intensity seem to my eyes coherent and clear, quite like a Francis Bacon introductory sentence. I have encountered these words often this semester, and last evening I realized that these seven words go beyond my Bacon analogy; these words, in that order, mean much more for my life than I have imagined.

I am cautious to admit such a statement. Hardly, if ever, do I feel a sense of connection, a sense of close mental, physical, and emotional proximity to any object, any person. When those connected moments do occur, other life experiences rudely interrupt and rigorously concern my mind. As a result, I lose the connection. I know that my reasons for teaching English and for pursuing advanced degrees in literature stem from the lack of connection I feel toward life and its parts. Literature always remained with me despite my changing self-concept and self-esteem; literature remained connected to me on every level imaginable when people could not understand. I categorize all of my life experiences as moments of connection or moments of disconnection.

I can recall a confession to my parents that resulted in a loss of connection. I was a sophomore in high school, and around mid-April I informed Mom and Father of my sexual orientation. I brought them into my bedroom and told them that I needed to tell them something very important. I think my parents were already on guard because I rarely invited them into my room, and I rarely told them something very important. Such monumental experiences did not happen to me in my family; they happened to my brother Justin who has learning disabilities and my sister Shanda who has celiac disease, a disease that does not allow her digestive system to dissolve wheat, rye, oat, and barley products. As they sat down on my bed, I took a seat in my reading chair. Then I told them.

I waited for responses. My mom responded: "You can't be a teacher if you're gay. You'll get AIDS and die." She may have said more, but her tears fell down her face as her hands covered her mouth so I could no longer hear her words. My father quickly added, "If you ever tell me about this fuckin' shit again, I'll hang you by your balls." Soon after they left. I do not know how to categorize nor do I wish to try to understand their leaving beyond the fact that they left my room. I do not blame them for their reactions or their ignorance toward my confession. While I did not expect them to be supportive right away, I expected them to ask more questions. They never did; my sexuality obstructed, and continues to obstruct, my connection with my parents.

I lost my connection with my favorite teacher too, but in a different way. Mrs. Bliss taught sophomore English for at least twenty years with great authority. She demanded careful thinking and precise solutions to every aspect of English. She taught us to remember details about every text and every author. I wanted to emulate her and I still do, at times, when I teach. In my mind, our deep affiliation began when we read Truman Capote.

Before any reading, Mrs. Bliss's students took notes on the author's biography. In her crisp, clear tone she informed the class that Capote was a homosexual. I expected her to tell us more because we had always learned how an author was connected to other people. Previously, she talked about Arthur Miller's various love interests as well as Shakespeare's family. She did not elaborate on Capote, but at least vocalized the word homosexual in a sophomore English class. She did not leave the classroom or comment in an ignorant manner like my parents. I knew a connection began.

Since she had spoken the word that I identify with in class, I felt that I could confide in her. On an April afternoon, I asked her to shut the door so we would not be disturbed. While she did honor my request, I think she sensed the situation's gravity and reacted accordingly. She added to that sense of privacy a large portion of secrecy as she shut the lights off and dropped the blinds. After I told her the already familiar story, I waited for her response. She spoke with a tone of tiredness and a tinge of sadness in her voice: "I am honored that you chose to tell me, but you have to promise me not to share the information with other people. High school is not the time for people like you. If the students find out, they will crucify you on the football field. Stay focused on your schoolwork." I sat still and took the words in.

At first I thought these words sounded like a sign of support, and I strongly wanted her to accept me completely and talk with me more about my life, but then I thought about the tone and the tinge in her voice. Life demanded so much of her as a sophomore English teacher, wife of a struggling farmer, and grandmother to a boy with absent parents. Why did I bother her with my coming out too? Maybe she did not feel the same connection that I did earlier that week? My questions immediately made me think about helping Mrs. Bliss with her work. I needed a way to take the focus of my situation and place the focus on another person. I am not sure why I felt that I needed to help her or that I owed her anything. Perhaps her articulation and careful delivery of "homosexual" made me want to thank her because she acted in the manner that I wanted my parents to act, or perchance her stress blocked her true reactions toward my coming out.

Mrs. Bliss and I remained in contact for the next two years because I graded her papers. I thought that was the least I could do for someone who spoke the word homosexual and whom I bothered with my coming out confession. Despite my consistent turnover rate of packets, quizzes, and examinations and detailed statistical summaries concerning missed questions, highest mark, and lowest mark, she never asked. Mrs. Bliss did appear less stressed due to my help, but she never brought up my sexuality again. Instead of doing so myself, I took her advice and did not make other connections, other lasting memories in high school. I focused on my schoolwork as I feigned survival and sameness. I followed her advice.

While Mrs. Bliss taught me that professional, not personal, relationships exist between teachers and students, her close colleague and confidante showed me more about classroom connections. Ms. Kratochvil taught junior English and everyone derided her. Students noticed when she came to school in white pants with traces of black dog hair, which reminded some immature students of pubic hair. Shortly after that incident, students called her "Ms. Crotchvil." They whispered in the hall after English class that her shirt came up again today, exposing her white belly, when she was speaking about Hester Prynne and her head slightly bobbled again as she wrote on the board. Ms. Kratochvil never overtly noticed or commented on these whispers and derisions. She remained focused on her teaching.

I talked with Ms. Kratochvil a lot and noticed that she never spoke of her personal life with anyone except Mrs. Bliss. I deducted from the computer page printout dog pictures and statistics that dominated her desk as equally as our essays did that dog breeding and dog showcasing deeply interested her. I wanted to talk with her about her personal life because few people had engaged her in conversation or had listened to her. No one, besides Mrs. Bliss, expressed care about Ms. Kratochvil's well being. I could be Ms. Kratochvil's confidante if she wanted. I never asked her about those pictures or statistics, but focused on my grasp and my understanding of American literature. (I could not bear a repeated Mrs. Bliss experience or another pile of papers to grade.) I gathered from the many times I saw her eating dinner alone and grading papers at restaurants that she did not have a significant other. I never asked why because I focused on developing my writing style for the Regents Examination. She was a pleasant and easily misunderstood woman like so many of the characters we read about in class: Hester Prynne, Arthur Dimmesdale, Roger Chillingworth, Ethan Frome, Mattie Silver, Zenobia Frome, and Huck Finn. Unfortunately I lacked courage at that moment to ask.

I think, or at least want to think that, I am becoming a lot like Ms. Kratochvil everyday, pleasant at times, but in the main easily misunderstood. I avoid, as she does, personal discussion about myself. I do not desire to bother others with my concerns that they can hardly fathom or honestly handle. I will happily listen to another's concerns, though. If I tell my students about my personal life, I risk front-faced comments on my appearance, idiosyncrasies, and possibly even my name. If I tell my students nothing, I keep a mystique about myself and need not acknowledge their comments concerning my person. I choose the latter because I tightly hold onto Mrs. Bliss's lesson about the teacher/student relationships. They should, I believe, remain professional.

While high school weakened my connection to people and place, I pursued three undergraduate degrees at SUNY Potsdam. Despite rarely encountering queer people, places, and ideas at Potsdam, I independently researched and wrote about queer topics like understanding Theognis of Megara's elegiac poems as an attempt to achieve equal love between adult men and adolescent boys. Also, I wrote on William Beckford's *The History of the Two Princes and Friends, Alasi and Firouz* as an example of an author consciously choosing to silence a homosexual narrative and publishing a queerly similar heterosexual narrative. While I was exuberant in my writing and research, formally presenting my research ruined more possibilities of connection. Few professors and classmates cared or commented. Maybe they were negotiating their own dealings and decisions with knowledge in both a professional and personal manner. Maybe I pushed too much. For certain, they did not connect with me.

At Potsdam I learned and now believe that the most worthy and beneficial connections involve literature and respect. A relationship based on literature and mutual respect will endure because understanding position, perspective, and point of view consumes time and energy. As the amount of time and energy increases my attachment to literature, my connection becomes stronger. So, I read. I read a lot. I am still alone, but the book that I hold in my hands respects my understanding of the world and loves me back. My books challenge me to contribute constantly to the university discourse. In keeping myself alone and reading, I find accepting invitations to socialize odd. When I am asked, I go out. I dance and laugh all night and more, but when I dance or laugh I wonder. Am I connected? I do not think so because connection, to me, involves more than physical activity for a few hours or a night; connection involves a total immersion into a person's life. I realize that this total immersion may never be possible or desirable and may appear scary and demanding.

I teach and pursue the field of English because I want students to learn about literature and respect as the true ways of connection. I need to encourage their minds to know more about the complexities of literature and life. I desire that they experience the uncomfortable moments of learning and the comfortable times of mastery. Ultimately, I want to change their minds, their brains by connecting them to literature and respect.

PART III

8

Not Fab Enough: Consumer Gay Identity and the Politics of Representation

Marcos Moldes

In the generation after Stonewall, gay bodies have had an increased presence in all forms of media representations. In print, entire magazines and newspapers devoted to gay issues have appeared and lesbians star on popular television shows like *Will & Grace,* or *Queer as Folk* these developments have often been touted as being a positive step forward in the struggle for gay empowerment. However, mainstream gay representation is not so straightforward that it can be seen as an entirely positive development. Although the emergence of mainstream gay media is often discussed as being an encouraging step forward for the gay rights movement, representations of gays and lesbians on television and in print are not necessarily a sign of universal acceptance for members of this community. Instead, they often represent the assimilation/co-option of a small segment of the ideal imagined gay and lesbian community, those who mirror in many ways the straight world of consumer subjects.

This consumer subject representation has become the stereotype of gay identity, as it is this image that is most often reproduced and consumed by all audiences. The stereotype that depicts gay identity as shallow and consumed by the latest gadgets and fashions is furthermore associated with affluence, whiteness and youth. Other than sexuality, these are the same identity markers of the ideal mainstream consumer to which television shows and advertisements in both broadcast and print refer. This gay subject has become the darling of advertisers: he is embodied in television shows such as *Will & Grace,* and *Queer Eye for the Straight Guy*. He is the ultimate, frivolous consumer. As an advocate for luxury purchases, he has come to be understood not just as any gay figure, but a universal gay figure, for he has dominated the media landscape with his presence. I use the male pronoun "he" for a very specific reason, the gay consumer subject of the mainstream media is, with few exceptions a male subject. For this reason this paper focuses mainly on the gay male community and how these images/representations fail to address systemic issues of exclusion. This does not mean that the erasure of trans/queer/lesbian communities from mainstream representation is not of great concern rather that a deconstruction of the gay consumer subject is the primary focus. This representation exists as a complicated and paradoxical figure in contemporary media. Historically homosexuality has been marginalized, constructed as deviant and policed heavily as an abnormality, yet its most recent media incarnations suggest a tenuous negotiation between economic co-option and marginalization. Mainstream media have adopted a very specific image of gayness that relies on consumer culture to validate it as a legitimate identity. Gay alternative media has, surprisingly, embraced this image of gay men, reinforcing the discourse of identity formation through product consumption that is central to the gay consumer subject. The gay press proudly showcases advertisements for products and services emblazoned with the image of this same ideal gay consumer.

fab magazine, a bi-weekly based in Toronto, is an example of a gay tabloid press that claims to provide an alternative medium to traditional discourses of gay identity, yet promotes mainstream images of the gay male body. The magazine provides local coverage about Toronto's gay community, and contains features about larger national and international stories from a gay perspective. The magazine also contains featured columnists, music and restaurant reviews, and a classified section that focuses on gay businesses and services. While *fab* represents a minority community, it does so by embracing and glorifying the normative images of the gay body that articulate the mainstream conception of gay consumer identity. This creates a contradiction at the centre of the magazine: one the one hand, it is a text that seeks to represent a minority community while, on the other, it mirrors a stereotypical construction of identity visible within mainstream discourse.

The images in the magazine are representative neither of the entire gay community nor of alternative approaches to health and beauty. Instead they focus almost exclusively on a very small segment of the community, one that is homogenous and increasingly one that has come to define a gay identity. Representations of this body can be seen throughout the gay landscape as it has come to encapsulate the way in which all media portray gay ontologies. That is to say that the gayness as a way of being is represented as a gay body that is limited to a small population of a broader and more diverse reality. I refer to this body in the singular precisely because of how homogeneous it is: while various models are deployed, they all resemble one another, so closely, I would argue, that they come to function as a visual template that others must conform to in order to be recognized as gay. This subject, although a minority, is still incredibly powerful by virtue of the fact that it occupies a privileged position in the media landscape: I argue that by thinking of the gay body represented in mainstream and advertising media as a disciplinary structure, it is possible to then understand how this representation is imbued with the power to create a very restrictive and exclusionary understanding of gay identity. This articulation of gayness excludes and erases those who do not conform to the standards set out by the mainstream and increasingly glorified by alternative media. I argue that this body is powerful because of its ability to be a coercive agent, which "forces" individuals to conform to strict criteria in order to be recognized and understood as gay subjects. This gay body, like the beefcake imagery first examined by Thomas Waugh, is characterized through its muscular and well-defined physique.

Similar to the pinup girls and cheesecake photography of the mainstream, beefcake photography was a phenomenon characterized through the use of provocative images that bordered on being erotic. This genre of photographic representation is a high point in gay erotic culture that belonged neither to the illicit pornographic underground nor to a "high art" regime but rather existed in a liminal space in-between the two (Waugh 176). These pictures, circulating under the auspices of being part of an athletic "jock" culture were in fact the fomentations of a gay body that glorified the fit and young bodies that were depicted in the images. Despite the fundamental disavowal of any sort of homosexual desire being part of the circulation of these images it is clear that they were part of the foundation on which modern gay identities and cultures were built (Waugh 177). This body symbolizes the ways in which capitalism has expanded itself into the realms of leisure, sport and erotic expression and has influenced gay culture in the process: through the commodification of the beefcake body (Waugh 191). By creating a template for a body that relies on capitalism to exist, images like that of the beefcake genre, or the gay consumer subject, are implicated in the relationship between capitalism and mainstream conceptions of the gay body.

I argue that the consumer gay subject cannot merely be seen as an extension of this cultural aesthetic. Beefcake photographs relied on the athletic body in order to pass through the censors that existed prior to the gay civil rights movement. By claiming to be inspirational material for men these photographs legitimized the pleasure of looking at male beauty and provided an outlet for male homosexual desire. This legitimization must have attracted, sheltered, and facilitated an important (if superficially invisible) gay constituency, a constituency that at that moment in history had few other outlets of expression (Waugh 188). However this body, which occupied a counter-cultural space during the pre-Stonewall era, is no longer the subversive tool of gay empowerment that it once was. Instead has become central to a mainstream understanding of gayness that is reductive and exclusionary at best.

The elevation and accommodation of this body out of abjection to a highly glamorized subject position is evidence of how the normative gay body has become a celebrated cultural icon. This body is an interesting site of analysis precisely because of how it has been raised up from the margins as an almost exclusively consumer subject.

Given that representations of gayness in both alternative print media and mainstream media have focused largely on a singular body this body has come to dominate the media landscape as a stand-in for the majority of articulations of queer identity. This image embodies the following characteristics: First, it is invested in representing the gay body as a consumer subject who articulates his identity through conspicuous consumption. Second, while considered to be universal in terms of representing gayness, this body is constituted by a highly exclusive construction of gayness that identifies a young, white, wealthy, slim, male body as the universal gay subject. This representation of identity is predicated on racial and class-based exclusion, as well as on other physical characteristics of bodies that do not conform to the rigid framework that regulates the dominant gay representation. The overwhelming use of this body to represent gayness—let alone queerness—is evidence of the refusal of most media to accept anything but a very narrow view of what it means to be an ideal, gay subject, that is to look like one who belongs within the gay community. This narrow depiction of identity is indicative of mainstream media's limited knowledge of the gay population.

The erasure of gay bodies that do not conform to the dominant representation constitute what I argue to be another category: the non-normative gay, or queer body. I refer to this category as non-normative precisely because it falls outside of the normative framework of the gay subject position. Examples include people of colour, the transgender community, lesbians, working class gays or people with disabilities, in essence, those that fall outside of the boundaries of the normative gay subject described above. By distinguishing between the normative and the non-normative bodies, I argue this allows for a consideration of how the normative body exercises power over the non-normative subject and comes to be considered the dominant subject in terms of representation. This results in an erasure of non-normative bodies and limits the discussion of gay/queer identities to an extremely simplistic and singular representation of identity that is rooted in consumer culture. While these two bodies occupy two distinct categories, they are obviously related and will serve as my principle distinction when discussing the representation of gay/queer identities. These distinctions are significant for the manner in which readers interpret, recognize and understand representations of a sexual/gender identity.

The non-normative gay body has been a largely ignored figure in gay magazines like *fab*; it is an unintelligible, queer body whose power lies precisely in its refusal to exist as a concrete identity category. In other words, the non-normative other escapes definition because it is difficult or impossible to attach a mainstream identity category to it. Because the non-normative gay subject's very nature renders it an elusive, complex body that defies a simplistic representation because it challenges familiar constructions and textual representations. The complexities that constitute the ontologies and epistemes of the non-normative other are simultaneously the strength and weakness of the queer subject position: both the gay and mainstream media largely ignore the non-normative other because of the difficulty that exists in labelling this diverse identity category. Coupled with this complication is the continued marginalization of queer bodies due to a lack, actual or perceived, of access to consumer culture. In the age of private enterprise and advertising-based revenue models, this perception makes the non-normative other a low priority for advertisers. Instead, representations of gay/queer bodies have focused almost exclusively on articulations of identity through simplistic consumer categories and the repeated use of the normative other as a universal representation of queerness. This representation emerges from both gay alternative media and mainstream media and has come to be considered what I call the normative Other regardless of how limited and exclusionary this representation actually is. The limiting nature of this representation presents an interesting set of contradictions with respect to understanding how this body operates as a culturally specific signifier. As a dominant image within both the mainstream and an otherwise marginalized culture, how does this figure participate in the displacement of other bodies that do not conform to normative identity categories? Does the act of displacement make this intelligible other a powerful body because of its ability to marginalize those who do not conform?

In order to understand the term "mainstream queer," it is important to recognize that mainstream representations of queer identity are often part of larger campaigns on the part of advertisers, transnational corporations and media conglomerates to gain the attention and favour of queer consumers. For example, In *Queer Visibility in Commodity Culture,* Rosemary Hennessey suggests that more recent gay visibility is not aimed at creating diverse discourses of queer identity, but rather at engaging lucrative and favorable markets for large corporations and for-profit ventures looking for new niche markets and consumers (112). Hennessey extends the discussion to examine how companies sought to promote themselves as gay friendly. "In the early nineties gay-friendly corporations like Levi Strauss, for example, reinforced the gender-flexible subjects its advertising campaigns promoted through gay window-dressing strategies by way of public relations programs that boasted of the company's progressive corporate policies for lesbians and gays" (Hennessy 138). In order to access the gay niche market, Hennessey claims that companies have sought to create bridges into the community through sponsorship campaigns, publicity and intense marketing to brand themselves as "gay positive" (113). These messages imply that through brand loyalty to gay-friendly companies, gay consumers will support companies that have helped empower gay men and lesbian women. The gay consumer is constantly encouraged to spend his/her way to liberation by supporting companies who donate money to gay organizations, extend benefits to same-sex partners and help sponsor Pride Parade festivities in cities across the world. However, drawing on the most famous example, the Coors family (of the brewery by the same name) simultaneously and actively supports anti-gay religious groups while also being the corporate sponsor for gay pride festivals (Bellant 50). Furthermore, the inclusion of gay men and women in mainstream consumer culture is not indicative of a broader move towards equal rights, but is instead merely the accommodation of a select elite who have been embraced as consumer subjects.

Gay media have also benefited from the desire of corporations to access gay and lesbian consumers and have been able to act as a bridge between the boardroom and the bedrooms of a community defined by sexuality by creating an image of queerness that shapes the climate of consumption. Several gay-oriented companies have become multi-national corporations by providing larger companies access and advertising expertise for tapping into the gay market. This process began on a broad scale during the late 1980s, which saw the beginnings of the acknowledgment of the gay consumer subject. Hester and Gibson identify that by the late 1980s, several corporations had begun to produce ads featuring well-known openly gay figures in publications that targeted gay men and lesbians. As gay minorities became more visible during the 1990s, major corporations (see endnote) began to actively target gay men as consumers, and companies[1] produced print advertising campaigns targeted specifically toward sexual minorities (Hester and Gibson). While some gay people have benefited from this discourse of empowerment through the marketplace, others have been shut out because of the classist discourse that is constructed from consumer subjectivity.

This facet of gay-themed media engages with a very specific construction of gay identity, and is one that can be directly linked to the conservative thrust of the post-Stonewall gay rights movement. This movement sought to promote the idea assimilation into mainstream culture, to be accepted as "just like everybody else" (Sender 77). By contrast, it is the concern of queer scholarship to consistently look at and challenge media representations that exist within the mainstream media and to resist images that misrepresent or limit queer identity. Queer scholarship also addresses the erasure of the reality of queer communities outside of its mainstream, white, middle-class members. Or, more precisely, gay communities must ensure that as normative gays are accommodated into mainstream society, the more radically queer project of questioning and challenging issues like heterosexism, patriarchy, and gender normativity is not abandoned.

While the emergence of queer representations in mainstream media should be considered a major development for the queer rights movement because it suggests that gaining visibility means acceptance, these representations of gays and lesbians on television, radio and in print are not necessarily a sign of authentic acceptance of members of the queer community. Acceptance into the mainstream as consumers is a questionable step forward for the queer community because it does not indicate a broader entrée within mainstream culture. Images that glorify queer consumption and promote the acceptance of the queer consumer do not address the systemic problems of homophobia and enforced normativity that continue to challenge and oppress diversely positioned queer community members. This is an attempt to harness the stereotype of the posh and sophisticated gay man, a man who is represented as the ultimate tasteful consumer. Acceptance into consumer culture is, characteristically, a redress for the disenfranchisement of those labelled as "other" (Chasin 39). The failure of consumer culture to redress the larger problems of the representation of queer sexuality, however, indicates the real lack of depth of consumer culture as a politics of identity since queer images are often homogenous and flattened into simplistic representations of hyper-consumption. This homogeneity proves that a broad acceptance of queers has not occurred, and that there has been a narrow and limited acknowledgement of the existence of a diverse queer audience.

Lisa Peñaloza, author of "We're Here, We're Queer and We're Going Shopping!" notes that the recognition of the queer market as a consumer group brings with it serious implications that are similar to using gender or race as niche markets (32). Advertisers have a long history of looking at minority communities as niche markets that need to be marketed to and thus accessed as potential consumers. Virginia Slims cigarettes, for example, is a product which was developed precisely for the female market with its slogan of "You've Come A Long Way Baby" and paired with images of the 1920s flapper woman, a figure who represents a progressive, and modern woman in American popular culture (Toll and Ling 172). African-Americans, another market that Peñaloza compares to gay marketing tactics, are consistently targeted by campaigns that offer low-cost products in television commercials (Henderson and Baldasty 103). The use of stereotypes, like the faux feminism and poverty deployed above, may define new markets but they ignore the complexities of identity politics by overlaying it with an image that has been structured around the act of consumption.

The rise of queer visibility in mainstream media during the early 1990s was coupled with the discovery of what advertisers dubbed the "Dream

Market." This notion of marketing nirvana was based on the assumption that gays and lesbians were a distinct consumer group with high levels of disposable income as compared to the heterosexual nuclear family (Peñaloza 10). The recognition of the queer community in mainstream television and advertising was also used as a way of integrating gay/lesbian/bisexual consumers into the larger consumer culture.

Upon the "discovery" of the gay consumer, advertisers immediately moved to market this subject as a site of tremendous potential for corporate bodies seeking to expand their consumer base. In order for this body to be co-opted, the gay marketplace was re-framed and portrayed in a way that was acceptable to neo-conservative mainstream media. Advertisers sought to "re-brand" gay bodies from being deviant to being sophisticated and chic consumers that should be emulated. While popular culture has a long history of appropriating elements of gay culture, it oftentimes did so without acknowledging the gay community from which a trend came. This appropriation has now shifted as a result of how the gay consumer has now been linked to an image of affluence and cosmopolitanism. Looking at the television show *Queer Eye for the Straight Guy*, for example, the five hosts, all self-identified gay men, are portrayed in a way that capitalizes on the premise of the show; that there is a perceived association between gay men and great style (Sender 137).

Marketers of mainstream products have praised the discovery of the niche gay and lesbian market and have sought ways to enter it. One of the methods used has been to create images of queer identity that is entirely upper class. Effectively, what has been manufactured and capitalized on is an elite queer consumer class that consists of a homogenous group of gay male and female bodies. While, this new surge of queer "friendly" images and texts in print and broadcast media have been viewed as positive accomplishments for queer politics, it is still important to question the constitution and validity of these representations. The linking of gay identity with an affluent consumer subject position is a myth that must be debunked since it problematically constructs an identity that, while empowering for a small group of queers (mostly affluent gay men) remains far out of the reach of the majority. Most importantly, we might ask how embracing this singular articulation of gay identity has affected the representation of those who do not adhere to the strict framework that constitutes this identity. What impact has the assimilation of a very small segment of gay culture had on the larger gay communities and its individual members? Finally, are these images perceived as being beneficial to the gay community solely because they are reproduced and repeated almost exclusively by mainstream media?

According to Chasin, there is no reason to think that financial profit amounts to either economic or political betterment for the queer community as a whole (44). Images of attractive Caucasian queers produce a mythology of affluence and broad acceptance. These images of good-looking, wealthy queer people support advertisers' efforts to market a product not only as queer-friendly and inclusive, but also as one consumed by the upper classes of the capitalist elite. Hennessey notes that the creation of the gay consumer depends on advertisers and their corporate clients creating a narrow, but widely acceptable image of gay identity that serves as a useful marketing tool to integrate the politics of queerness into a marketing niche (137). These images act as a symbol of the limited acceptance of queerness, one that embraces the stereotype of the queer consumer and provides limited access to mainstream media by allowing queer bodies to exist merely as stand-ins for all consumers. Therefore, it is easy to argue that representations of queerness have little to do with the acceptance of the queer community by the mainstream. While queers continue to operate on the fringes of political and social acceptability, mainstream media have created images of gay consumers void of a significant political or social articulation.

Larry Gross contends that the lack of queer visibility and visible resistance is due to the hegemony of the mainstream mass media. Gays and lesbians, along with other sex-gender "undesirables" (such as drag queens or the transgender community), lack representation because they are a challenge to the established order (Gross 409). This inability of queer identity to create media representations that are then picked up by the mainstream for itself represents a problem that, while not exclusive to queers, is perhaps more blatant and pronounced (409). According to Gross, the problem with queer television programming is that it does not speak to the gay community since it is not representative of it, but is, instead, intended to be consumed by a heterosexual mainstream audience (410). The poverty of images and representations used by mainstream media are symptomatic of the need for an alternative media that offers alternative portrayals of the queer community. Because current mainstream representations of queer identity are all based on the representation of a gay consumer subject, there is a clear need for representations of queerness that include what the market has deemed undesirable by virtue of its *difficulty* as a vehicle for consumption.

I argue that the capitalist constructed gay subject, in this case represented by *fab* magazine, is in fact the contradictory subject position produced as a result of the same set of capitalist contradictions. Although capitalism has allowed for identities to exist outside of the heterosexual family structure, it has also reduced these identities in terms of representation since there are no well-established or validated ideologies to support them. Capitalist gay identity, represented by the homogenous image of gay affluence, has become a hegemonic subject position—in effect, an essentialized, subject position that erases and ignores anyone who does not conform to its version of gayness. The *fab* queer represents two distinct and contradictory images of the gay subject that is constructed and construed as being a threat to the nuclear/heterosexual family, which ultimately limits the gay subject to a singular construction. This essentialized subject makes the gay body a convenient and recognizable body—one that can be invoked and interpellated by the mainstream. Representing gay subjectivity in this simplistic manner is problematic in two distinct ways: first, this representation of a universal queer requires that the magazine becomes normative in the sense that it excludes articulations of queerness that do not resemble its own definition. Secondly, the essentialized gay subject allows for the targeting of those who are recognized as gay subjects—that is to say this subject position turns bodies into visible targets for disciplinary power. The magazine does this by identifying a very specific queer reader and then selling this readership to advertisers. Bodies that not conform to this implicit ideal are almost entirely erased from the pages of the magazine thus leaving few options for those who articulate a queer identity differently. The message is: either conform (if even possible to conform), or be ignored.

In *Addressing the dyke: Lesbian Looks and Lesbians Looking* Reina Lewis and Katrina Rolley make several observations about fashion magazines and the lesbian audience that I extend to my own analysis of *fab* magazine. First, that the milieu of fashion magazines is a world without men, both the producers and readers of the text are assumed to be female (Lewis 179). Second, that fashion magazines are fundamental to a socially prescribed and formative feminine experience, this experience is one that tutors women in consumer identity (179). Finally, that sexuality is fundamental to the production, consumption and content of the magazine which links the magazine's construction of feminine identity to sexuality (179). These characteristics are parallel to those found within *fab* magazine: the milieu is distinctly male, it seeks to tutor its audience in an identity steeped in consumerism and sexuality is fundamental all aspects of the magazine.

Arguably, *fab*'s representations of race are problematic because of its over-representation of white bodies and under-representation of bodies of colour. This lack of racial diversity in the magazine's visual rhetoric aids in reinforcing gay identity as a distinctly white identity, a phenomenon that needs to be deconstructed, as it is part of the systemic and documented racism found in the gay community. I will be referring to this specific representation of white identity by drawing on Richard Dyer's definition of whiteness, a term that he describes as being understood as a racial category and a specific racial wealthy socio-economic class (46). In order to operate within the realm of gay identity (the one that is constructed by the visual rhetoric of *fab*'s cover images), it is necessary to adhere to the dominant racial identity associated with gay masculinity: whiteness. By linking gay identity to a racial/economic subject position, the covers engage in a coercive act that excludes gays of colour.

Issue #5 (see Figure 1 at the end of the chapter) of *fab magazine* is an example of the racism and sexualization faced by people of colour in gay media. The cover image features two men, one white and the other black, wearing wigs made out of marabou feathers fashioned to resemble the Afro-puff hairstyle. The white model is standing over the black model and is completely nude except for the aforementioned wig (made out of black feathers) on his head with the black model's head positioned to obscure his penis from the viewer. His hands are on his hips and he is looking downwards presumably at the black model that is positioned in a submissive and deeply problematic position.

This positioning of the two models is incredibly sexualized as well as laden with connotative messages about racial dominance. There is a clear power dynamic occurring between the two, one that replicates colonial narratives of white dominance over racial bodies and the attendant sexualization of black bodies. Because the black model is positioned to cover the white man's genitals his identity in this image is completely linked to the penis of the white man. This image contains stereotypical, colonialist representations of the black body: a submissive black man who is being dominated by a white overseer and a linkage between black male identity to the penis. Thus the image draws on normative (racist) representations of the black body, a body that is being dominated by a powerful white model and is sexualized by standing in for the penis. I argue that this image lacks any sort of playfulness that could be interpreted as a camp reclamation or critique of race, instead that this image replicates stereotypes of the black body.

Looking at the headline on the cover "The Black and Blue Issue" (#5), it becomes clear that there is a double meaning at play here: first, a reference to the BDSM/Leather community—a community that uses terms such as "master" and "slave" to denote power positions within their relationships. Barthes identifies a relationship between text and image that is useful for understanding how this headline functions in relation to the image of the two models. For Barthes, text is often attached to a photograph to further connote the image, "to quicken it with one or more second order signifieds" (Barthes 25). In this case the headline reinforces the idea of a master/slave relationship between the two models through the linking of the image to a subculture that appropriates this terminology as a form of sexual expression.

I argue that the linking of this community to problematic depictions of race and power is an attempt to obscure the problematic racial constructions of gay identity. This also attempts to sanitize the realities of racial inequality in the gay community behind the consensual power relationships that occur within the BDSM/Leather community. The second meaning that can be read from this headline is what the colours black and blue are often associated with: bruises that are the result of physical violence. This linking of violence to a black body that is being physically dominated by a white body is laden with messages, two of which I will use as examples. First, an echo to the colonial violence of the slave trade in which black bodies were often turned "black and blue" through the savage beatings they faced at the hands of white slave owners. This image places that oppression and that history of displacement into a sexualized context: the use of a sanitized image where two beautiful models come to stand in for an unequal power relationship rooted in several hundred years of oppression erases the realities of colonial violence. Secondly, the association of black bodies to represent physical danger unless contained and controlled. The image can be read as reinforcing and encouraging the oppression of black bodies under the guise of safety: if not for the white authority figure in the image that dominates and controls the black threat, the black model may turn the reader "black and blue." The use of black men as a phobic object, a site inscribed with fear and anxiety, has a long history rooted in colonialism. By continually reproducing a discourse that constructs blackness as a threat that has been, and must continue to be, contained brutality against black men both physically and in a socio-economic context is justified (Mercer 134).

The sexualization of the black body on the cover of the magazine can also be seen on the cover of issue #61 (see Figure 2). Initially this image seems to represent the black body in conjunction with almost all of the other *fab* models: as young, muscular and well toned. However, unlike many of the other models found on the magazine's cover this model is entirely nude with one hand grasping at the backdrop material attempting to cover his genitals. The entirely nude model is positioned to appear as though he grasping at his surroundings in an attempt to cover himself from the viewer. Unlike other cover images where the sexualized body looks directly at the viewer, his eyes are averted and his head is bowed slightly. This image reads as coy submission, shame and, unlike the other cover models, this model does not look back at the viewer. Instead, he is positioned to evade the onlookers as he tries, in vain, to cover himself up. His body is positioned not as an active participant in the looking, he is not welcoming the audience to look, rather he is being looked at.

It is not the sexualized image of the black body that I find problematic, rather, it is how the black model's sexuality is represented. This image is an example of how racial Others are sexualized as a submissive sexual object for consumption by a white audience. Representations of blackness are constructed in reference to the white audience, either as a sexual object or as a violent and phobic object that needs to be contained. Gay black sexuality in the case of issue #61 is not represented as a point of pride but rather as being shameful and something that makes the model hesitant to acknowledge the presence of the viewer. Furthermore there is a huge disparity in terms of representations of the black body in general, one example is the lack of consistent representation: out of all of the cover images between issue #56 and issue #81, only issue #61 has a cover that features a model who is a visible minority.

The use of a model of colour that emulates the normative gay body points to some of the complexities that exist in the relationship between image and text on the cover pages of *fab* magazine. The depiction of a model that visually conforms to most of the norms of the disciplined gay body (except the presupposition of whiteness) and in conjunction with headlines that mark the model as existing outside of the gay community are examples of these complexities. This cover becomes a case in point of how the text uses racialized bodies both as an inclusion, in terms of actual physical presence, and as a simultaneous exclusion when the entire cover image is critically examined. The visual representation of a model of colour can be seen as breaking away from the dominance of the normative gay body, but the linguistic message then reinforces the racial boundaries that constitute this body. Borrowing from the language of Barthes once more the linguistic message directs the reader to the correct ideological messages within the image. Although an initial response to the inclusion of a racialized Other on the cover of the magazine can be seen as a moment of progressive racial politics the headline is evidence that this cover merely reinforces the status quo. Specifically, the gay Other becomes an object of curiosity that the magazine places on the cover in order to be consumed by the white gay audience.

Issue # 195 (see Figure 3) serves as an excellent example of the idealized gay consumer subject: white, young and physical well defined. The writing on this cover is particularly interesting because of how it functions in relation to the image. The model constitutes an image that is clearly a reinforcement of the young buff body as the central subject of gay identity. He is fit and attractive, bare-chested and holding a dumbbell in his hand that has been positioned to appear as though he was in the middle of doing bicep curls. This subject is presented to the reader alongside several written messages the first of which is literally inscribed into his body. On his chest the phrase "0% Fat" is written in a stencil style font and the headlines of the magazine that accompany this image are positioned to the left of the model. The first headline reads "In praise of body fascism" and the second poses the rhetorical question "Buff bodies beat bigotry?"

This cover exemplifies how the disciplined body is constructed as a powerful subject in *fab* magazine not only through its overrepresentation, but also through the way that the magazine establishes it as the "correct" embodiment of gay identity. The body of the model that is linked with the headlines inform the reader of how it *should* serve as the template for all gay bodies. The model's torso is branded with the phrase "0% Fat" in a stencil style font. This font also has an aesthetic that bears a striking resemblance to the font often associated with the brand used to mark livestock. Arguably the use of an aesthetic that resembles a livestock brand evokes messages of cowboy masculinity, and although the model is the one being branded the message within the brand claiming his body to be "0% Fat" is one that (literally) marks the body as being powerful and masculine.

In "Fatvertising: Refiguring Fat Gay Men in Cyberspace" Jason Whitesel notes that body image is one of the major influences of the demarcation of socio-cultural boundaries (93). Fat, and visual representations of fat are the means by which bodies are regulated in terms of their acceptability; to be labelled as fat is a clear demarcation of undesirability in the eyes of *fab* magazine. Therefore the absence of fat on the model and the branding of the model as being fat-free is, arguably, a means by which this image seeks to reify and empower the model via the brand on his chest. Whitesel argues that fat bodies are often associated with stereotypical feminized features and that these features are represented as being a threat to masculinity and the disciplined muscular body (Whitesel). Therefore, in an attempt to conform to normative representations of the male body images like the cover of issue #195, publications like *fab* magazine adopt restrictive representation of gayness. This not only links the body to the disciplined gay subject visually but also create a linguistic justification for this linkage. This justification is visible in two of the other headlines on the cover of the issue and is evidence to how images and the written word function in relation to each other.

The first headline, "In praise of body fascism," is fairly explicit in terms of the initial message about the gay body—it is clearly a reference to the model positioned immediately to the right of the headline. What is less explicit however, is that this headline advocates adopting a fascistic sense of exclusion for bodies that cannot or do not conform. Furthermore, the word fascism, an incredibly loaded and powerful word in itself, evokes images of a racialized identity that places bodies like this model's in a dominant power position. Indeed, the model fits well within the Aryan youth model of Nazism, and while the appropriation of this aesthetic by a gay text does produce a moment of subversion the magazine is using this image to further a politic of exclusion.

The second headline poses the question "Buff bodies beat bigotry?"—a question that further pathologizes bodies that the magazine deems to be insufficiently "buff." Additionally, this question also establishes the following problematic line of thinking: if buff bodies beat bigotry, then a means to beat bigotry is to be "buff." Buffness is a trait associated with idealized masculinity and therefore it is not a means by which bigotry is overcome, rather it is a means by which bigotry is shifted to the non-normative gay subject, a subject that the magazine clearly has little interest in representing. I argue that the question posed in this headline can largely be read as rhetorical due to the presence of a disciplined gay body as the cover model for the issue. By establishing the disciplinary gay body as *the* means through which homophobia can be challenged, a new culture of exclusion is circulated by the magazine. Furthermore this headline clearly argues for conformity to the normative gay subject that the magazine has constructed: it implies that if all of *fab*'s readers were to embrace this body template then the problem of bigotry could be overcome.

The glorification of the normative gay subject represented as having embraced a fascistic sense of body politics as a tool in the fight against bigotry becomes a convoluted representation through which the magazine deems this subject to be the "correct" mode of identity. There is no mention on the cover about how the muscular normative body participates in the reinforcing of racist, sexist and deeply class-based discourses of gay identity that are exclusionary to the majority of gay-identified individuals. The gay community as imagined by these exemplary narratives suggest that the magazine is a space that is demarcated for a very specific male subject.

In the case of *fab* magazine, the deployment of this body is especially problematic given that it claims to be a text written by and for the gay community but largely ignores the majority of the community in its use of "representative" images. The imagined gay body thus becomes one that is delimited to embracing the consumer subject, yet *fab* also advocates that this embrace is an articulation of authentic identity. This body, however, is one that mirrors mainstream media's representation of gay men and merely reaffirms the political and social disenfranchisement faced by a majority. The *fab* gay man is then implicated in a disciplinary structure that expunges queer politics and queer activism from current discourses of gay representation. This consequence is a result of how the *fab* body is imbued with a form of power that makes him the recognizable gay subject.

The *fab* body, therefore, can be understood to operate as a disciplinary regime precisely because it is recognized as a distinctly gay one. The recognizable body is developed specifically by texts like *fab* that construct and market an intelligible gay body to advertisers and audiences. This body appeals to both groups for separate (albeit related) reasons: for audiences, the intelligible body represents recognition and partial inclusion into mainstream discourse. The body itself is marked using the aesthetics and language that mainstream media has denoted as indicative of a gay male identity. Discourses of "chic" and "fabulousness" imbue it as a desirable subject and texts like *fab* glorify this body; this is, within the realm of both mainstream and gay media this is an image to strive for, emulate or otherwise to achieve. A gay subject will want to become a *fab* subject in order to be understood.

Although the normative gay body lacks real political power and indeed does not articulate a desire for political or social change in its representations it is afforded a great deal of cultural capital. Imagining gay men to be a group of urban, affluent, white men absolves society from addressing chronic issues of homophobia, racism, poverty and social exclusion. If the normative gay body exclusively represents gay identity, then gayness by extension is comprised entirely by a group of consumer-frenzied men with large amounts of disposable income. The myth of gayness then absolves both mainstream and gay culture from dealing with the issues that affect our communities. This is not a simple matter of gay people versus straight people, these issues intersect lines of sexuality and include issues of race, gender and economic class. The myth of the normative gay body attempts to obscure these problems by presenting a sanitized and "safe" image of gay identity. As long as the normative construction is dominant and fits within the ideals of hegemonic masculinity then there is no need to seriously consider efforts to counter heteronormativity, or prejudice. If gay identity is based on consumption and affluence then suddenly homophobia is not a problem nor is the drive toward larger political and structural change.

In the post-Stonewall, post-*Will & Grace*, post-*Queer as Folk* landscape of contemporary gay culture this image functions as a filter to those do not (either by choice or by inability) conform to its rigid construction of gayness. There is a need for gay culture to recognize that the boundaries of exclusion that this image consistently reinforces are no longer productive ones. These boundaries no longer create safe spaces for the exploration of homoerotic desire; rather they are boundaries that exclude a majority of gays from participating in culture.

NOTE

1. According to Hester and Gibson (2007), these companies include: Miller, Coors, Absolut, Stolichnaya, Ford, Subaru, Toyota, Volvo, American Express, The Gap, Banana Republic, and Wyndham Hotels (2).

BIBLIOGRAPHY

Barthes, Roland. *Camera Lucida: Reflections on Photography*. New York: Hill and Wang, 2010.

Bellant, Russ. *The Coors Connection: How Coors Family Philanthropy Undermines Democratic Pluralism*. Boston: South End, 1991.

Bowes, John E. "Out of the Closet and into the Marketplace: Meeting Basic Needs in the Gay Community." *Journal of Homosexuality* 31.1–2 (1996): 219–44.

Bruhn, John G. *The Sociology of Community Connection*. New York: Springer, 2005.

Chasin, Alexandra. *Selling Out: The Gay and Lesbian Movement Goes to Market*. New York: St. Martin's, 2000.

Dyer, Richard. *White: Essays on Race and Culture*. New York: Routledge, 1997.

Foucault, Michel. *Discipline and Punish*. New York: Vintage, 1979.

Goltz, Dustin Bradley. "Laughing at Absence: *Instinct* Magazine and the Hyper-Masculine Gay Future?" *Western Journal of Communication* 72.2 (2007): 93–112.

Gross, Larry. "Out of the Mainstream: Sexual Minorities and the Mass Media." *Remote control: Television, audiences and cultural power*. Ed. Ellen Seiter, et al. New York: Routledge, 1989. 130–49.

Henderson, J. J. and G. J. Baldasty. "Race, advertising, and prime-time television." *The Howard Journal of Communication*, 14 (2003): 97-112.

Hennessy, Rosemary. *Profit and Pleasure: Sexual Identities in Late Capitalism*. New York: Routledge, 2000.

Hester, Joe Bob and Rhonda Gibson. "Consumer Responses to Gay-Themed Imagery in Advertising." *Advertising and Society Review*, 8.2 (2007).

Johnson, Carol. "Heteronormative Citizenship and the Politics of Passing." *Sexualities* 5.3 (2002): 317–36.

Mercer, Kobena. *Welcome to the Jungle: New Positions in Black Cultural Studies*. New York: Routledge, 1994.

Mitchell, Danielle. "Producing Containment: The Rhetorical Construction of Difference in Will and Grace" *The Journal of Popular Culture* 38.6 (2005): 1050–68.

Peñaloza, Lisa. "We're Here, We're Queer, and We're Going Shopping! A Critical Perspective on the Accommodation of Gays and Lesbians in the Marketplace." *Journal of Homosexuality* 31.1–2 (1996): 9–41.

Sender, Katherine. "Queens for a Day: *Queer Eye for the Straight Guy* and the Neoliberal Project." *Critical Studies in Media Communication* 23.2 (2006): 131–51.

Shugart, Helen A. "Reinventing Privilege: The New (Gay) Man in Contemporary Popular Media." *Critical Studies in Media Communication* 20.1 (2003): 67.

Toll, Benjamin A., and P.M. Ling. "The Virginia Slims Identity Crisis: an Inside Look at Tobacco Industry Marketing to Women." *Tobacco Control* 14.3 (2005): 172–80.

Waugh, Thomas. *Hard to Imagine: Gay Male Eroticism in Photography and Film from Their Beginnings to Stonewall*. New York: Columbia University, 1996.

fab!
MAGAZINE
Mid-September 1994
Issue 5
$2.50 Newsstands
The Black
& Blue
Issue

fab
Toronto's Gay Scene Magazine
Issue No. 61 April 5, 1997
This Just In
BOYS ARE BACK pg 4 • GETTING NOSTALGIC pg 16 • "REAL

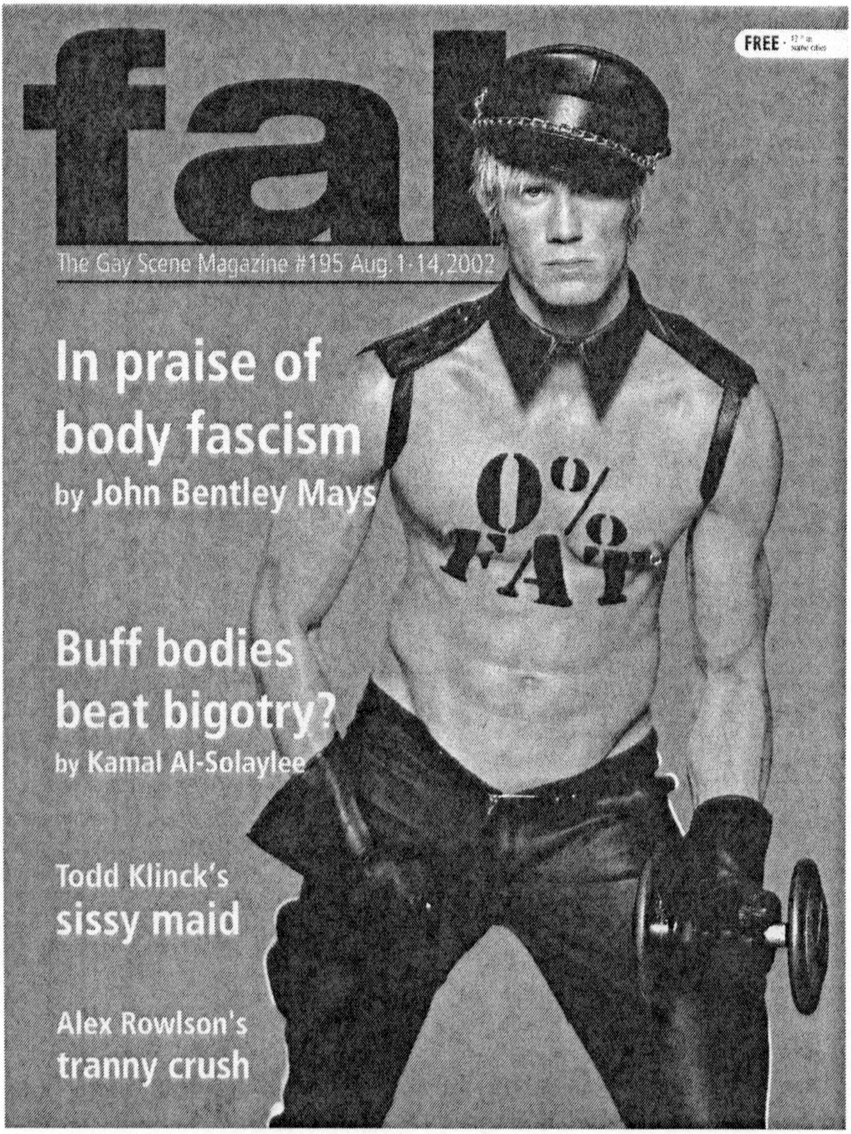
fab
FREE
The Gay Scene Magazine #195 Aug. 1-14, 2002
In praise of body fascism
by John Bentley Mays
0% FAT
Buff bodies beat bigotry?
by Kamal Al-Solaylee
Todd Klinck's sissy maid
Alex Rowlson's tranny crush

9

Don't Dream It, Be It: Cult(ure), Fetishism, and Spectacle in *The Rocky Horror Picture Show* and *King Lear*

Brianne Colon

I do not think my mother has ever forgiven my father for taking me to see a Halloween showing of *The Rocky Horror Picture Show* when I was twelve years old. Standing on Granville St. at midnight outside the Plaza, the endless array of fishnets, pubic hair and sequins seemed to just plain make sense. As I watched the lovely men in—what I learned later were corsets, I immediately became part of this group—that *Rocky Horror* obsessed cult that surfaces but once a year, but never truly lies dormant. Once inside the theatre, the spectacle surrounding the performance made every other cinematic experience up until that point in my life seem lacking. The live concurrent re-enactment of the film, offensive call-backs and audience-encouraged dance and participation gave a new meaning to the words worship and performance. From that evening on, I could not wait to relive the thrill of the performance, to worship once again the characters onscreen, and to give myself over to this group.

Although I am almost positive that this was not the night I realized I was queer, to this day I cite it as the night wherein queerness became a possibility. As such, this chapter will consider the ways in which belonging to a group means ascribing to certain prescriptions surrounding individuality. It will also examine the flipside of what happens when one fails to worship said prescriptions. When younger, *Rocky Horror* functioned as a way out of my wayward teenage sexuality into a type of asylum. Also, theatre in general became a place wherein spectacle took over reality, if only for a moment, making it a very alluring venue. More recently, the act of writing this chapter has, for me, been an act of queering myself within the academic eye. As *The Rocky Horror Picture Show* has remained a very under-researched text, I decided to use my queer Rocky whore status to exploit its peculiarities, as well as the peculiarities of worship in general. Why discuss Shakespeare when one can consider Shakespeare as socially relevant to cult film? By comparing *The Rocky Horror Picture Show* and *King Lear*, two texts separated by more than four-hundred years, this chapter will argue that despite seeming discrepancies, there is a degree of continuity between the ways in which these texts are worshipped as cultural artefacts, as well as the worship portrayed within the texts themselves. Although they seemingly might have very little in common, each text's treatment of the group dynamic underscores a society built on a false network of worship, instead of any real power. While the form this worship takes often varies, this chapter will highlight three levels (or even methods) of worship: culture, fetishism and spectacle.

Given that one of these texts was written in Elizabethan times and the other during the late twentieth-century, one of the auxiliary claims of this chapter, then, is how little the social customs and public consequences of worship have changed. Despite an increasingly secular and pluralized society where pop culture has supplanted religion, the monarchy within each text displays similar levels of public, private and social worship—leaving the modern liberal State apparatus and the pre-modern monarchy as sites of fetishistic devotion. Both Lear and Frank lose sight of their actual power due to their own self-idolatries—or what I am calling their "fetishized notions of self." Finally, as both *King Lear* and *Rocky Horror* circulate within their respective audience communities with similar degrees of fetishism, I will look at the external worship directed at the texts themselves. While their public reception may frequently separate them in terms of high and low culture, both texts exist within their own spectacle, and I will examine how these spectacles manifest themselves, and even suggest how they both participate in a larger cultural coming out.

In *Keywords*, Raymond Williams explains how the term "culture" comprises many different levels: it is first, "a general process of intellectual, spiritual and aesthetic development"; second, "a particular way of life of either a people, a period or a group"; and third, "the works and practices of intellectual and artistic activity" (32). What is inherent in these three levels of culture is the sense of the group, and even Freud suggests that "every individual is virtually an enemy of culture"(6). Culture is a site of public worship, relying on group consensus. It becomes linked with worship in the idea of reverence. Culture is certainly a force which temporarily coheres the opinions of a group—either private or public—into one semi-confined conceptual space. It depends on a group consensus which informs the direction of that group's reverence.

Just as culture is threatened by external factors, its popularity of public opinion often wanes. As both texts show, culture can quickly shift in and out of public favour, and its borders so often blend into that which we deem "cult." Like its parent term, cult is simply a part of one culture ascribing to—honouring—a particular set of ideals, which often have negative connotations. As with culture, though, we see the idea of closed group formation being of prime importance. We see an example of culture's inconstancy in the way in which culture and cult move in and out of one another in *Rocky Horror*. When Brad and Janet arrive at "the Frankenstein place" (*The Rocky Horror Picture Show*), they quickly learn that they "have arrived on a rather special night. It's one of the Master's affairs" (*The Rocky Horror Picture Show*). They then witness a rather totemic performance of the "Time Warp," a group dance involving nearly everyone within the castle, with the notable exception of the two newcomers. That the film begins in Brad and Janet's world—outside the castle—and then moves into the castle and this dance aids in constructing life inside the castle as a cult built around strange sexual rituals. Janet faints repeatedly throughout the "Time Warp" and exclaims afterwards that "it seems so unhealthy here . . . I want to go"(*The Rocky Horror Picture Show*). When confronted with this sexual cult she is unwilling to partake. Her horror of the Frankenstein place manifests itself as a revulsion to this particular form of group worship, therefore solidifying it as a cult in her perception as an outsider.

Later in the film, though, we see a shift in cultural perspective. Once Janet has experienced sex and life within the castle, she admits to having "tasted blood and [wanting] more" (*The Rocky Horror Picture Show*). Although initially repulsed and scared by life within the castle, she grows increasingly fond of the sexual liberation encouraged therein and begins to adopt it as a positive way of life. For Janet, the group worship no longer represents a cult and she internalizes the group's ideals as part of her own, thus becoming a part of that which once repulsed her. Just as Janet's perception shifts, the movement from the exterior of the house to the interior takes shape, as well. It is no longer Brad and Janet through whom we view the castle's actions; the couple becomes an essential part of them, too. At the end of the film, they participate in a theatrical performance staged by Frank wherein they are both dressed in corsets and drag make-up. They agree to "give themselves over to absolute pleasure . . . swim the warm waters of sins of the flesh" (*The Rocky Horror Picture Show*) and, most importantly, hail Frank as their leader. That their transformation from outsiders to insiders within the castle culminates in a cultural performance—the "Floor Show"—shows that they now appreciate life within the castle and belong to the group residing within it. They are perpetuating Frank's rule through their own actions and are participants in the group consensus of what constitutes culture within the household.

This reflects the film's reception, as well. While I entered that theatre a twelve-year-old first-timer, I left as part of a distinct new group—one that subscribed to *Rocky Horror*'s ideals and would definitely be back next Halloween for more. Therefore, Brad and Janet's transformation from outsiders to insiders within the castle's domain reflect the journey that each Rocky whore must take in order to become enveloped within the film's culture.

In *King Lear*, we see another shift in cultural perspective, this time from culture to subculture. While a subculture is quite different than a cult, they are still similar in that they are both relatively small in size, are usually associated with negative connotations, and require a larger culture within which to exist. Dick Hebdige defines subculture as "the expressive forms and rituals of . . . subordinate groups" (2). We see this type of group subordination from those who reject the dominant culture in *King Lear*. Whereas the beginning of the play opens with a display of Lear's culture, embodied within the rituals of the court, the loyal members of Lear's society that stay with him after Goneril and Regan have reneged upon their sentiments create a kind of subculture—they are literally branching off from the larger initial culture of their society. Forced outside where it is "storming still" (Shakespeare III.ii), Lear is now attended by just his Fool and Kent, as his daughters have ejected him from their societies. This is perhaps more of a conscious subculture on the part of Kent and the Fool—as they *choose* to be subordinate to the larger culture now in power (i.e. Goneril et. al.) and instead, continue to revere Lear. Nonetheless, they comprise a subculture in their subordination. Much like *Rocky Horror*, those that begin within the larger umbrella of culture—Janet and Brad as "normal, healthy kids" (*The Rocky Horror Picture Show*); Lear as reigning member of his culture—break off into subordinate groups before the text is through. The shift shown in both texts reflects that this group level of worship is infallible only as much as humans are constant.

Our worship within a larger cultural setting relies heavily on knowing how to worship at all. One of the ways in which we first participate in worship is through fetishism. This brings us to our second level of worship portrayed within the texts: the personal, or private. While it may seem problematic to link such a subconscious method of idolatry as fetishism to worship, if we reconsider our earlier definition, we see how the two ideas cannot help but overlap. Fetishism presupposes a certain level of adoration with the fetish-object—it is a fetish-object strictly because of this adoration. While Frank creates Rocky as a fetish-object, the scene following Rocky's birth shows Frank chasing his creation around the set and kissing his ankles and the ground upon which Rocky has just walked. Rocky might be nothing more than a fetish-object for Frank—a mere representation of the "perfect specimen"(i.e. Charles Atlas)—but he is still honoured and revered, with Frank even going so far as to throw a birthday party for him later in the film.

As fetishism is a fundamentally individualistic response to a perceived lack, followed by an overcompensation, it is a type of solitary worship borne out of an even more solitary fear. Linked with idolatry in its tendency towards worship of a material object, it differs from its parent concept in that it is not a group form of worship, but instead a solitary desire. Although the Marxian use of the word implies certain public implications, each individual consumer is responsible for this larger public implication; they must individually internalize the desire in order to outwardly produce it, therefore turning the focus back onto the individual. In Freudian thought, "fetishes . . . characteristically want to be beheld—to 'be held' close by, or even reattached to the body of the fetishist" (Mitchell 194), showing an intimate relationship between the fetishized and fetishizer. This idea of relationality is important, as it is in all of idolatry; yet, here, it is undeniably more individual in expression.

As previously alluded to, the Marxian concept of the term—commodity fetishism—is also a solitary form of worship, even though it is mediated through larger social implications. The concept implies an individual desire to be the sole possessor of a particular item. Unlike its Freudian cousin, though, the Marxian term involves exterior social intervention, as it is society which dictates that which becomes a commodity (and the union of these individual desires that organizes capitalism). Although this seems to exclude the Marxian concept of fetishism from the aforementioned "private level of worship," at its core, commodity fetishism works through individual overcompensations: "Fetishism for Marxists involves a confusion between [use value and exchange value]. . . . The miser hoards his or her gold as if it had value in itself, not realizing that it is valuable only in terms of what it can be exchanged for"(Hawthorn 69). It is true that the miser covets his gold because of its social value. Yet it is his own confusion between the wealth and value that cements the gold as a fetish object. Its actual value is gone, replaced by the miser's own sense of value. "Value, therefore, does not have its description branded on its forehead" (Marx 167); it is dependent upon each individual to create this value him or herself. Therefore, while commodity fetishism depends upon society as a whole to establish these commodities, it is on an individual level where we see this worship truly take shape.

Despite their respective psychoanalytic and economic implications, Freudian fetishes and Marxist commodities both function on this personal level, and both seem to arise from a sense of fear inherent in the fetishizer. Robbins and Myrick explain the fetish from a psychoanalytic point of view, highlighting Singer's findings in relation to film theory: "[the fetish is] 'a material object that functions as a penis-substitute, a surrogate for the mother's missing penis . . . the fetish assuages castration fear and restores the female body as good rather than as threat,' by recasting the female body as phallic"(271). By casting this everyday object on the site of the mother's missing phallus, "[the fetish] remains a token of triumph over the threat of castration and a protection against it"(Freud 154). This overcompensation succeeds in that the object of worship allows the boy to continue believing "in his mind the woman *has* got a penis, in spite of everything"(154). It is fear as a manifestation of the transference of desire. Much like in psychoanalytical theory, the fetishizer within a Marxian framework of fetishism also worships out of a type of fear, or desire run amok. If we return to our earlier example of the miser and his gold, there comes a point when the miser stops worrying about simply having gold, and becomes more worried with not having enough of it. He begins to overcompensate, and consequently, hoard.

It is not surprising that from these overcompensations arise individual difficulties. In fact, it is this personal level of worship that ultimately winds up destroying both Lear and Frank within their own societies. Both men develop fetishized notions of self, which cause them to lose sight of their actual power. In *King Lear*, we see these fetishistic principles at work almost immediately in the opening scene. To the crowd, Lear states:

> Know that we have divided
> In three our kingdom; and 'tis our fast intent
> To shake all cares and business from our age,
> Conferring them on younger strengths while we
> Unburdened crawl toward death. (I.i.39–43)

Although he believes he shall "shake all cares and business from [his] age," he does not see this as a means of stepping back from his power. It is here that Lear begins to embody many of the qualities of the Marxian miser. He is dividing his land, true, but not before divorcing the land's value from its actual price. No longer does the land attain its value based on its use. Instead, it becomes the site of his own fetishized ideals and a part of his State mask—a concept to which we shall soon return.

Jack Amariglio and Antonio Callari note that, "the attribute of economic rationality implies that individuals treat the objects they possess and trade as quantities that can be calculated"(208). Just as Lear's rationality is in question throughout the entire play, we see here a question of economic rationality in what Lear demands in return for the land. Before his court, he says

> Tell me, my daughters
> (Since now we will divest us both of rule,
> Interest of territory, cases of state),
> Which of you shall we say doth love us most,
> That we our largest bounty may extend
> Where nature doth with merit challenge. (Shakespeare I.i.50–55)

He plans to divide his land according to which of his daughters comes forth with the greatest avowal of love. Although one could argue that here he is fetishizing his daughters' love, I am arguing that it is only his daughters' *proclamations* of love with which he is concerned. He cares not for the love itself, merely the words in place of it. He is exchanging the proclamations of love for land, and also, his acceptance. Lisa Freinkel calls the fetish "a metonym"(117), and these proclamations of love are functioning as just that: a part of the supposed whole. When Cordelia does not respond willingly to her father's wishes, instead saying "nothing"(Shakespeare I.i.91), he "[disclaims] all [his] paternal care,/ propinquity and property of blood"(I.i.116–17). Her refusal to partake in her father's fetishized method of rule is what bars her from his society.

We see a similar fetishization in *Rocky Horror*. When Brad and Janet are "shown to their separate rooms" (*The Rocky Horror Picture Show*), Frank takes this opportunity to test their loyalty to him. What follows is an exchange of sex for social acceptance. Frank enters Janet's room first, disguised as Brad, and proceeds to lure Janet into sleeping with him. After he has triumphed over Janet, he re-enacts the exact same scene with Brad, triumphing over him, as well. That Frank uses sex as a means of enacting his acceptance of these newcomers shows, once again, this lack of (economic) rationality. As we learn that Frank has undertaken a similar process with almost each character in the movie it becomes clear that within this house, sex is the only guaranteed method of Frank's acceptance. These sexual exchanges within the house are "an 'agreed upon' system of calculation that is followed by all agents [of trade]" (Amariglio 214). Just like Lear's economic irrationality surrounding land and proclamations of love, Frank's fetishized notions of self lead him to develop this scandalous routine in order to separate those who are with him, and those who are against him.

But what is it that causes each man to confuse his power with love/sex? How is it that these fetishized notions of self manifest themselves with each ruler? Michael Taussig discusses the idea of maleficium, or State fetishism, and shows how "we so casually [identify] 'the State' as a being unto itself, animated with a will and mind of its own . . . something much greater than the sum of its parts"(218). He continues by outlining the concept of the State mask, which he develops by drawing upon Philip Abrams's ideas: "The State is not the reality which stands behind the mask of political practice. It is itself the mask which prevents our seeing political practice as it is [and] it starts its life as an implicit construct" (219). The idea of the mask is comparable to the fetishized ideas that Lear and Frank have of their own power. We see this in *Rocky Horror* through the staging of the floor show, wherein Frank dresses and makes up each of the characters to look nearly identical to himself; he remakes them as idols in/of his own image, displaying his self-idolatry at work.

As Frank regards himself as the illusory pinnacle of power in the castle, Lear is also heavily reliant upon his own State mask. He believes that by keeping his title as king he will retain all of his respect, men, and lifestyle. He fails to see that being a king is more than mere title. This is why scenes later, when Goneril and Regan both refuse to support Lear's "insolent retinue/ [who] do hourly carp and quarrel, breaking forth/ in rank and not-to-be-endured riots" (I.iv.204–6), he is angered and shocked. He separates his actual diminished power as a king with no land from his only-in-name title as a figurehead king. Likewise, Frank believes that by ruling his house through absolute pleasure, everyone within his house will practice what he preaches and nothing more. We see this position in Frank's response to discovering Janet and Rocky together. He tells Rocky "I made you and can break you just as easily" (*The Rocky Horror Picture Show*). Frank's sexual prowess is enveloped within his personal State mask. Those (perceived) subordinate members of his household are threats to his State mask and therefore power within the house.

Although we see these "attacks" on Lear's and Frank's fetishized notions of rule, it is not these attacks alone which cause each man to crumble. Instead, it is the iconoclastic blows dealt to their fetishized notions of home/ State rule, which others are wont to interpret as idolatrous. In each text, we see two succinct examples of iconoclasm—or, image-breaking. As "idolatry and iconoclasm . . . [remain] vital categories of cultural criticism"(Morgan 130), it is not surprising that elements within each monarch's society inevitably turn on him. "Scholars have linked iconoclasm to the polemical construction of idolatry and rigorously historicized both concept and practice as polemical formations embedded in social conflict" (116). Therefore, when such social conflict arises in each text, the iconoclasm that surfaces becomes nothing more than a negative response to the idolatry present in the house. Moreover, it is clear that the attacks in *King Lear* and *Rocky Horror* are directed at Lear's and Frank's fetishized ideals, or self-idolatries—thus fixing this idolatry in said ideals.

As previously mentioned, Cordelia responds "nothing"(I.i.91) when Lear demands of her a proclamation of love. She is attempting to shatter her father's over-exaggerated notion of self and exclaims that "I love your Majesty/ [a]ccording to my bond, no more nor less" (I.i.94–95). Unlike her father, she does not confuse power and love, and unlike her sisters, cannot pretend to do so. By saying "nothing" to her father, she is enacting a type of iconoclasm, as she is going against Lear's fetishized notions of self. There is no violence associated with her act, which is perhaps what makes it such a fruitless attempt on her part: Lear retains his over-exaggerated perceptions of self and denounces her "as a stranger to my heart and me" (I.i.118), demanding her to "[h]old thee from this for ever"(I.i.119). We see this motif continue when Kent questions Lear's banishment of Cordelia. Kent tells Lear that "your youngest daughter does not love you least"(I.i.155), at which point Lear gives Kent five days before he must "turn thy hated back/ [u]pon our kingdom"(I.i.178–79). That both Cordelia's and Kent's attempts at humbling their king fail shows how ineffectual mere words are against Lear's self-idolatry. None the less, such iconoclasm sets forth a chain of reactions leading to the eventual iconoclastic destruction of Lear's State mask.

Much like Cordelia's and Kent's words, Frank is also dealt an iconoclastic blow by Columbia and Janet. After he has unveiled and animated his creature—Rocky Horror—he seeks praise from those within his kingdom. When asked their opinion, Riff-Raff and Magenta exclaim that Rocky is "a credit to [Frank's] genius" and "a triumph of [Frank's] will"(*The Rocky Horror Picture Show*). Just like Goneril's and Regan's false proclamations of love, Riff-Raff and Magenta are simply saying what Frank wants to hear. When Columbia is questioned, though, she states that Rocky is simply "okay" (*The Rocky Horror Picture Show*), an opinion which is in direct contrast to Frank's own notion of his genius. Similarly, Janet responds that she "[doesn't] like men with too many muscles" (*The Rocky Horror Picture Show*), to which Frank exclaims that he "didn't make him for [her]" (*The Rocky Horror Picture Show*). Although these attacks are non-violent, they trigger feelings of anger and rage in Frank, which are caused simply by members of his retinue not conforming to his own self-idolatry.

These scenes differ tremendously from each monarch's second encounter with iconoclasm. In the second instances, the attacks are much more violent and, consequently, successful. They manifest themselves through each man's fetishized notion of home, or way of life. Lear believes that his previous rule and way of life shall continue even once he has given away all the land, but Goneril and Regan refuse. They do not want their father's fetishized rule to continue now that he holds no legitimate power. Goneril urges Regan to "pray you let us hit together;/ if our father carry authority with such disposition as he bears,/ this last surrender of his will but offend us"(I.i.307–9). The women carry out this intent when "his knights grow riotous, and himself upbraids [Goneril]/ on every trifle"(I.ii.6–7). Their refusal to partake in their father's fetishized method of rule is what leads to the eventual iconoclasm of outright rebellion, one that stops just short of patricide.

This iconoclasm takes shape over a number of scenes and begins when Goneril attacks her father's way of life within her own castle:

> Here you do keep a hundred knights and squires,
> Men so disordered, so deboshed, and bold
> That this our court, infected with their manners,
> Shows like a riotous inn. (I.iv.244–47)

Instead of allowing him to maintain his method of habitation, she asks him "a little to disquantity your train" (I.iv.252). Refusing, he takes his train to his other "daughter,/ [w]ho [he is] sure is kind and comfortable" (I.iv.309–10). The idea of comfort here relates to the idea of home. Whereas Goneril is not allowing him to proceed in the manner to which he is accustomed, Lear's confidence that Regan will have no problem succumbing to his every will and demand shows just how fetishized and self-aggrandizing his notions of home are. Much like the missing phallus "that the little boy once believed in and . . . does not want to give up" (Freud 152–53), Lear would rather disown another daughter and deny the reality of his situation than admit that he is no longer in utmost control. This denial fails Lear, however, when Regan demands him to "bring but five-and-twenty . . . to no more/ [w]ill I give place or notice" (Shakespeare II.iv.247–48). With nowhere left to turn, and forced to face the storm outside, he realizes that his image of home is forever broken. That both of his remaining daughters force him to give up seventy-five of his men is what finally shatters Lear's self-image. His idea of home, comfort (and the illusory locus of power that comes with it), is destroyed beyond repair.

Just as it is Lear's two eldest daughters that inevitably turn on him and deliver the fatal blow, Frank is dealt a similar blow by members of his most inner-society, specifically his two "loyal" servants. In his paper on iconoclasm, David Morgan is quick to note that "when an idol falls, its place does not long remain vacant . . . [a] rival is often quickly erected" (115). In Frank's second major encounter with iconoclasm, Riff-Raff and Magenta attempt to completely shatter Frank's State mask and take power of the household. However, when faced with Riff-Raff proclaiming that he is now "the new commander, [Frank] now [is his] prisoner" (*The Rocky Horror Picture Show*), Frank seems to remain calm. A sense of calm falls over him and he sings "I'm going home" (*The Rocky Horror Picture Show*) to a crowd of imaginary monarchs. Much as Lear is able to retain his fetishized notions of self even in the face of certain political desolation, Frank is able to ignore the reality of his situation by focussing on this idea of home. Once again—and for the last time—we see his fetishized notion of self delude him into misunderstanding the reality of his situation. At the end of the song, he opens his eyes only to discover that there is, in fact, no one there. It is then that the iconoclasm takes its full effect. Up until this point, Frank fixates on his return to his home planet, Transexual. That he actually projects his political importance onto delusions of grandeur echoes *King Lear* in that each man has trouble grasping the reality of the situation. And when they do finally grasp it, it is owing to the threatened notion of home.

In each case, it would seem that the further they get away from home, the more they crave it. This binaristic approach to an object—in this case "home"—displays one key characteristic of psychoanalytic fetishism: "Affection and hostility in the treatment of the fetish—which run parallel with the disavowal and the acknowledgement of castration—are mixed in unequal proportions in indifferent cases, so that the one or the other is more clearly recognizable" (Freud 157). Here, a sense of fear—or desire—creeps into "fetishism" once more. As much as the fetishist worships a particular item, there is also a repulsion; it "is a vision that both pleases and petrifies, as if the price of delight were destruction" (Freinkel 115). This reluctant relationship with an object so desperately craved is one indication that a fetishized relationship with said object exists. This reluctant relationship is also what pushes Lear and Frank over the edge, instigating their delusions and consequent madness. Once Lear recognizes that his idea of home remains with Cordelia—the daughter whom he disowned on account of her non-participation in his fetishistic game—he is overcome. His madness manifests itself through the realization of damage wrought by the fetishized ideals he earlier refused to give up. His confusion is seen in his reunion with Cordelia: "Where have I been? Where am I? Fair daylight? / I am mightily abused. I should e'en die with pity / To see another thus. I know not what to say" (Shakespeare IV.vii.52–4). This realization is accompanied by remorse. He calls himself a "foolish fond old man" (IV.vii.60) and the Doctor counsels Cordelia that "[t]he great rage/ [y]ou see is killed in [Lear]" (IV.vii.78–79). No longer is he the raving monarch worshipping his own mask of power; he is reduced to his use-value, which is not much owing to his advanced age.

Although much shorter in length, Frank's realization is equally maddening. Instead of realizing that he has built his mask of power upon nothing, he loses something much more important: his life. After his sentimental "I'm Going Home" number, he opens his eyes to the sound of Magenta's mocking tone: "how sentimental" (*The Rocky Horror Picture Show*). When Riff-Raff continues with "and all so presumptuous of you" (*The Rocky Horror Picture Show*), we see their iconoclasm take effect. Frank begins to shuffle himself up the stairs and away from Riff-Raff's ray gun, realizing that not only is he not going home, his previously loyal servant is now going to ensure that he stays there "in spirit" (*The Rocky Horror Picture Show*) only. Not only has he been denied access to his home planet of Transexual, his home within the castle is threatened as well. He is no longer able to support his method of (self-) idolatrous rule, as Riff-Raff and Magenta iconoclastically take his power away from him. The desperate attitude that affects Lear is reflected in Frank's attempted flight and seeming madness. That both men literally embody this State mask is furthermore what leaves them so (personally) vulnerable to attack. They see themselves as the sole source of power within their societies, which causes them to create a spectacle of themselves by attempting to force their personal opinions on those around them.

Just as Frank's and Lear's fetishistic masks are the driving factors within their societies' perception of culture, this relationship between culture and fetishism seems to present itself in this very idea of spectacle: our third level of worship. I have deemed this third level "the social" as I believe it manifests itself through the interaction between culture (a more public form of worship) and fetishism (the more private, or personal of the two levels). Up until this point, we have seen the ways in which these public and private levels of worship manifest themselves separately in *Rocky Horror* and *King Lear*. What happens when the two are combined, however, is precisely what Guy Debord is talking about in *Society of the Spectacle*. Debord views "the spectacle [as] the present model of socially dominant life" (6). It is "not a collection of images, but a social relation among people, mediated by images" (4). He explores the ways in which spectacle brings people together as well as its functions and constituents. His emphasis on Marxian theory throughout his text reflects the commodified position of the "viewer"(the one experiencing, participating in and creating the spectacle) and the "viewed" (the basis for creation). He notes that the spectacle's "first phases of the domination of the economy brought into the definition of all human realization the obvious degradation of *being* into *having*" (17). As with our earlier discussed idea of hoarding, once again we see this type of commodity fetishism which attaches itself to certain socially dominant objects and ideals. It is consequently "both the result and the project of the existing mode of production" (6), enveloping both the viewer and the viewed within one symbiotic space.

The degree of socialization associated with the spectacle—this "group" worship mediated through individuals—becomes reflected throughout various contingencies, or layers, of society. One of the most interesting paradigms that Debord suggests in his paper comes early on, and establishes this layered perspective. He says that the spectacle "presents itself simultaneously as *all* of society, as *part* of society" (3). This all/part dynamic is reflected in the very basis of spectacle itself. The spectacle is *all* of society in that spectacle consists of that which reverberates throughout an entire society. Whether or not we are participants in certain aspects of the spectacle, our discussion thereof and immersion therein suggests a preoccupation—either deliberate or reluctant. The spectacle also is *part* of society in that it depends on individual and personal relations—even fetishism—in order to perpetuate its saturation of daily life. Therefore, while this dynamic may seem rather contradictory, it is precisely this contradiction which defines the spectacle's nature.

We see this all/part dynamic of the spectacle at work in the opening scene of *King Lear*. The crowd is gathered to witness Lear's division of land, a very political function, reflecting the "model of socially dominant life" (Debord 6). After Lear presents his fetishized notions of rule, each part of his society is forced to react in one way or another, these private reactions reverberating through all of society. That the text's plot concerns itself with each character's acknowledgment of Lear's self-indulgent ways reinforces Debord's all/part theory, as each character must acknowledge Lear's actions individually, as well as culturally. In the spectacle "one part of the world *represents itself* to the world and is superior to it. The spectacle is nothing more than the common language of this separation. What binds the spectators together is no more than an irreversible relation. . . ." (Debord 29). Lear stands before his court and attempts to decide its future. Even though Kent may disprove of Lear's decision to disown Cordelia, he begins his disapproval with words of praise: "Royal Lear,/ [w]hom I have ever honored as my king,/ [l]oved as my father, as my master followed" (I.i.142–44). Debord discusses "the common language of this separation" and in this exchange between Lear and Kent, we see how the spectacle is the thread through which these two individuals relate. It is the only way in which these individuals might relate to one another—their only source of common ground. Therefore, while the spectacle is, indeed, all of society, that it must be honoured and upheld by its individual participatory members is how it can likewise be considered a partial representation of that society.

Rocky Horror also portrays this all/part dynamic in its representation of social worship. Directly following the end of "Sweet Transvestite" and Frank's departure, everyone gathers upstairs for yet another spectacle: the birth of Frank's creature, Rocky Horror. Once again, Frank establishes himself as the pinnacle of power within this scene: he positions himself before the sole microphone in the room and begins his preliminary speech. He announces to everyone that "[he has] the knowledge to life itself" and that "tonight is the night [his] creature is destined to be born"(*The Rocky Horror Picture Show*). Much like in *King Lear*, this one scene's actions become the basis upon which the rest of the text is based. Once "born," Rocky Horror is immediately labelled as a sex object, for it is clear that Frank has built him to be "good for relieving [Frank's] tension"(*The Rocky Horror Picture Show*). This, combined with Frank's heavily sexualized influence, causes Janet to later seek out Rocky as a sexual partner. She is both internalizing and enacting the larger spectacle in her own personal pursuit of pleasure. The spectacle therefore manifests itself as both all and part of society within Frank's mansion.

Even the full title of the film suggests its position as a type of spectacle unto itself and we see this in the external worship associated with the film. While initially created for the stage as *The Rocky Horror Show*, O'Brien's original title is maintained with the insertion of the word "Picture" for the film version. As we are now more than aware that the spectacle functions as a "social relation among people, mediated by images" (Debord 4), this insertion of the word "Picture" is not at all surprising. We have seen how the spectacle is both the basis and the result of ruling society, and Debord implores us to consider how it is that "reality rises up within the spectacle, and the spectacle is real" (8). Just as the reality of Lear's political decisions in the opening scene dictate the rest of the play, and Frank's assumption of power is reverberated throughout the house, the participatory nature of the spectacle reflects the ways in which both texts are and have been worshipped in their historical trajectories.

Just as Frank's lifestyle is idealized and perpetuated within the film itself, the audience develops a relationship with the film and the characters through live performances. Purdie remarks on how at these live performances, "the audience participation takes basically four forms. Firstly, the audience dresses [up as the film's characters] . . . [S]econdly, they also perform dances and dialogues as these occur in the film . . . [T]hirdly . . . *Rocky Horror* audiences also carry and use a set of objects . . . [And] the fourth . . . the dialogue the audience maintains with the film throughout its showing" (175–76). By assuming the characters' modes of dress, the audience participates in the spectacle, causing reality to rise up within the overall spectacle—life mimics the images onscreen. By participating in the dance numbers and dialogue, the spectacle occurring onscreen becomes the spectacle occurring off-screen as well. That the characters' reality becomes the audience's reality, as well, reflects precisely how the spectacle manifests itself within the confines of the theatre. Although this can be applied to theatre in general, the extent to which the audience voluntarily accepts the characters' reality in *Rocky Horror* is perhaps what sets it apart from most other films.

Purdie notes that the dialogue maintained by the audience throughout the film is "perhaps [the] most distinctive element" (176) of the audience participation, and it relates back to Debord's all/part dynamic. Although one may only get to participate in the full *Rocky Horror* experience once a year, this dialogue relies heavily on each individual participant's willingness to learn said dialogue on his or her own time. It is only by worshipping the film on a personal level that one can, in turn, worship it on a public level. While bringing toast, cards, rice, water-guns and the rest of the props does not take long, cultivating the dialogue takes many hours of practice, as there are call-back lines for almost every line in the movie. There are certainly differences in opinion when it comes to certain call-backs, and participants are encouraged to come up with their own, but without learning the appropriate dialogue ahead of time, this dialogue would simply cease to exist. Therefore, as we have seen, the spectacle of *Rocky Horror* is both *all* of the *Rocky Horror* society worshipping this text, as well as the *part* of this society which takes the time to participate in the spectacle outside the theatre itself.

While there is undeniably a difference in the external worship directed at *King Lear*, we nonetheless see the way in which Shakespeare has become a spectacle unto himself. As Garber says, "Shakespeare as fetish has . . . become the ideology of our age" (177). She reminds us that "those who inveigh against mixing high art with popular culture would do well to remember that Shakespeare himself began as popular culture, not as the icon of high art he has become today"(8–9). Not only was there a "popular" status associated with Shakespeare in the early modern era, there is also a popular status associated with him now. He is among the most widely-read English playwrights of all time, and his plays' continuous performances at festivals devoted to his work suggest that he is often revered as a type of divinity within the English canon. Even those who do not agree with this opinion are forced to find more proof against his divine status than they ever would have to for it. Garber remarks that "if not God, then Shakespeare, who amounts to a version of the same thing" (168). Debord suggests that "the spectacle is the moment when the commodity has attained the *total occupation* of social life" (42) and we see this in Shakespeare's saturation of the English canon. He is worshipped—respected, honoured, studied—above the level of almost all other playwrights, which is spectacular in its own rites. Therefore, while attending a Shakespearean performance is not the same as attending a live performance of *Rocky Horror*, both events move beyond simple theatrical experience and participate in the creation and maintenance of the their respective spectacles.

Rocky Horror fans are encouraged to "do the Time Warp again" (*The Rocky Horror Picture Show*); Twenty-first century Shakespeare fans are invited to participate in four-hundred years of historical context, all the while experiencing culture in one of its most (currently) prestigious forms. Although I have created three distinct categories of worship in culture, fetishism, and spectacle, there are no hard and fast rules that keep these ideas from overlapping. Throughout the course of writing this chapter, the difficulty that arose in the attempted separation of these three levels of worship became the uniting thread that held them together. As they all describe methods of worship—particularly methods of worship surrounding performance—it is not surprising that despite my best efforts to keep them distinct, the categories have no choice but to blend into one another.

This brings us back to the beginning of this chapter and the ways in which our movement between groups is equally fluid. If we once more consider the ways in which Frank's and Lear's lives unravel, we see how it is very much a process of self-revelation for each man; some might even say a process of coming-out. Although it might seem difficult to place Frank anywhere *near* a closet, let alone in it, both men's fetishized notions of self keep them from presenting their "real" selves to the larger public. Once they do dissolve their masks, however, they are forced into new groups—groups outside the specific scope of power. That both texts exhibit near-parallel examples of internal worship and are equally spectacular in their external worship reflects that while differences in historical context, style and audience reception inevitably separate them, *The Rocky Horror Picture Show* and *King Lear* share more than just a place in this chapter: they share the stage in a complex history of performance devotion and devotion to performance.

BIBLIOGRAPHY

Amariglio, Jack, and Antonio Callari. "Marxian Value Theory and the Subject." *Fetishism as Cultural Discourse.* Ed. Emily Apter, and William Pietz. London: Cornell UP, 1993. 186–216.

Anobile, Richard J., ed. *The Official Rocky Horror Picture Show Movie Novel.* Scr. Jim Sharman and Richard O'Brien. New York: A&W Visual Library, 1980. Print.

Becker, Howard. "The Culture of A Deviant Group: The 'Jazz' Musician." *The Subcultures Reader.* Ed. Ken Gelder and Sarah Thornton. London: Routledge, 1997. 55–65.

Bevington, David. *This Wide and Universal Theatre: Shakespeare in Performance, Then and Now.* Chicago: Univeristy of Chicago Press, 2007.

"Cult." *Oxford English Dictionary.* 5 November 2007 <http://dictionary.oed.com.proxy.lib.sfu.ca/cgi/entry/50055591?query_typ=word&queryword=cult&first=1&max_to_show=10&sort_type=alpha&result_place=1&search_id=C7rO-4jM9I5-27859&hilite=50055591>.

Dawson, Anthony B., and Paul Yachnin. *The Culture of Playgoing in Shakespeare's England.* Cambridge: Cambridge UP, 2001.

Debord, Guy. *Society of the Spectacle.* Detroit: Black and Red, 1983.

Freinkel, Lisa. "The Shakespearean Fetish." *Spiritual Shakespeare.* Ed. Ewan Fernie. London: Routledge, 2005. 109–29.

Freud, Sigmund. "Fetishism." *The Complete Psychological Works of Sigmund Freud.* (V.21). Trans. James Strachey. London: Hogarth, 1961. 152–58.

Garber, Marjorie. "Shakespeare as Fetish." *Symptoms of Culture.* New York: Routledge, 1998. 167–77.

——. "Symptoms of Culture: An Introduction." *Symptoms of Culture.* New York: Routledge, 1998. 1–14.

Hawthorn, Jeremy. "Fetishism." *A Concise Glossary of Contemporary Literary Theory.* 2nd ed. London: Edward Arnold, 1994. 69–70.

Hebdige, Dick. "Introduction: Subculture and Style." *Subculture: The Meaning of Style.* London: Methuen, 1979. 1–5.

Marx, Karl. "The Fetishism of the Commodity and Its Secret." *Capital: A Critique of Political Economy.* (V.1) Trans. Ben Fowles. New York: Vintage, 1977. 163–77.

Mitchell, W.J.T. "Totemism, Fetishism and Idolatry." *What Do Pictures Want?: The Lives and Loves of Images.* Chicago: University of Chicago Press, 2005. 188–96.

Morgan, David. "The Violence of Seeing: Idolatry and Iconoclasm." *The Sacred Gaze: Religious Visual Culture in Theory and Practice.* Berkeley: University of California Press, 2005. 115–46.

——. *Idols of the Marketplace.* New York: Palgrave, 2001.

——. "Culture." 5 November 2007 <http://dictionary.oed.com/cgi/entry/ 50055634?query_type=word&queryword=culture&first=1&max_to_show=10&sort_type=alpha&result_place=1&search_id=pTuJ-Iws9eU-13879&hilite=50055634>.

——. "Worship. 1 April 2008 <http://dictionary.oed.com.proxy.lib.sfu.ca/cgi/entry/50287317?query_type=word&queryword=worship&first=1&max_to_show=10&sort_type=alpha&result_place=3&search_id=kpEN-NI9Kev-7215&hilite=50287317>.

Purdie, Susan. "Secular Definitions of 'Ritual': The *Rocky Horror* Phenomenon." *Theatre and Holy Script*. Ed. Shimon Levy. Brighton: Sussex, 1999. 171–90. Web.

Robbins, Betty and Roger Myrick. "The Function of the Fetish in *The Rocky Horror Picture Show* and *Priscilla, Queen of the Desert*." *Journal of Gender Studies* 9.3 (2000). 269–79. Web.

Shakespeare, William. "King Lear." *Three Tragedies: Hamlet, Macbeth, King Lear*. New York: Scholastic, 1970. 249–383. Print.

Sharman, Jim, dir. *The Rocky Horror Picture Show*. Perf. Tim Curry, Barry Bostwick, Susan Surandon, Little Nell, Richard O'Brien. 1975. Videocassette. Twentieth Century Fox, 1992. VHS.

Taussig, Michael. "*Maleficium*: State Fetishism." *Fetishism as Cultural Discourse*. Ed. Emily Apter, and William Pietz. London: Cornell UP, 1993. 217–47. Print.

Williams, Raymond. *Keywords: A Vocabulary of Culture and Society*. New York: Oxford UP, 1985. Print.

10

Suddenly Last Semester: What Tennessee Williams' *Suddenly Last Summer* Taught Me About the Queer Dis-ease

Bradley Houston Lane

> "Of course one can feel queer. There are feelings involved in the self-perception of 'queerness,' a self-perception that is bodily, as well as bound up with 'taking on' a name. But these feelings are mediated and they are attached to the category 'queer' in ways that are complex and contingent, precisely because the category is produced in relation to histories that render it as a sign of failed being or non-being."
>
> —Sara Ahmed, *The Cultural Politics of Emotion*

I am standing in the men's room down the hallway from my shared office. I have been there three times already in the past hour so that I can scratch in private. Two weeks before the end of the semester, and my skin is on fire. Hives? Nerves? The nurse at the health center was not sure, but I've been given lotion to spread over my trunk and legs. The itching has been keeping me up nights, so I've been sleepy during the day when I should be awake, writing.

Moving to the Midwest to begin a doctoral program was a risky decision for me. I had been happy living where I was, with a full circle of friends and a nice income from a variety of teaching jobs. By mid-November, I can't remember the reasons that convinced me over the summer to go through with this move. The only thing I wish now is that I were further south, where, even in winter, the air is more humid and my skin wouldn't be so dry or red. At least I'd be able to sleep there.

The nurse also suggested that my body was not doing a good job of fighting off infection. My immune system was "compromised," I think she said, probably due to a high level of stress. I wondered what "compromised" means exactly. I didn't even know I was sick.

* * *

As the quote from philosopher Sara Ahmed that opens this chapter suggests, the word "queer" itself can provoke discomfort, both for those who employ it and for those who are interpellated by or within it. Judith Butler attributes this source of discomfort to the historicity of the discursive practice governing "queer." Building directly upon Derridean formulations of citationality, Butler asserts

> If the term "queer" is to be a site of collective contestation, the point of departure for a set of historical reflections and futural imaginings, it will have to revise that which is, in the present, never fully owned but always and only redeployed, twisted, queered from a prior usage and in the direction of urgent and expanding political purposes, and perhaps also yielded in favor of terms that do political work more effectively. ("Critically Queer" 14)[1]

In other words, contemporary citations of "queer" derive political power from that term's discursive history, according to Butler. Moreover, Butler sees the deployment of the term "queer" alongside a simultaneous critique of it as politically necessary and as a part of the practice of activism. As I use "queer" self-critically and self-consciously, I work from Butler's assumption that one may certainly claim "queer" for political purposes, but one must also affirm the very contingency of "queer" at the same time (Butler, "Critically Queer" 16). That very assumption influences the spirit in which I write, for I want this essay to be a queer experience for the reader and the writer, an experience that can perhaps provoke a relation to queerness that is itself (appropriately?) queer. To infect others with such a queer condition, I resort to a reading of the circulation of queerness as a contagious form of affect in the adaptation of Tennessee Williams' *Suddenly Last Summer* into a 1959 film. In my analysis, queer phenomenology and psychoanalysis provide a theoretical and methodological background that is rendered askew in crucial moments through instances of my own autobiography. Therefore, in addition to tracking queer discomfort, then, this chapter is also a textual montage that incorporates moments of my own queer discomfort in academia into an academic analysis. I do this deliberately to blur the boundaries separating my own queer body, the body of this essay, and the queer bodies about which I theorize.[2] In other words, you have been forewarned: what follows is a genealogy of my own queer dis(-)ease.[3]

If queerness is an emotional state, "feeling" queer makes for a peculiar kind of embodiment. In her analysis of the cultural politics of emotion, Ahmed complicates understandings of mind and body, surface and boundary. For Ahmed, emotions are not located 'in' bodies; rather, emotions shape the surface of bodies by creating boundaries and by orienting bodies toward or away from each other: "emotions create the very effect of surfaces and boundaries that allow us to distinguish an inside and an outside in the first place" (*Cultural Politics* 10). Queer bodies are those particularly unruly bodily surfaces that resist social, political, and especially sexual norms. Ahmed writes expressively of how norms function like repetitive strain injuries on bodies, making lasting bodily impressions that limit future movement. Moreover, Ahmed's notion of "orientation" is pivotal to her discussion of queerness as she considers how queer bodies are oriented toward certain bodies and away from others through poses that make those bodies appear misshapen, over-contorted—yes, even *twisted*—to most eyes. Ahmed subsequently explores "queer" as a feeling of discomfort, connecting heteronormativity to a kind of culturally inscribed public comfort that reflects back the couple form most people inhabit as a social and moral ideal. As Ahmed writes of heteronormativity, "comfort is very hard to notice when one experiences it" (147). Queer, then, becomes a kind of discomfort, a *dis*-orientation in which one's body feels awkward or out of place.[4]

As Ahmed shows, queerness as *deviation* from straightness takes on multiple levels of signification then. As "queer," one may deviate from heteronormative life-lines temporally or spatially, and in any number of manners. Perhaps one can be ill-at-ease in one's skin and be queer as a result, especially if the discomfort one experiences is the hallmark of feeling queer feelings themselves.

Orientation, disorientation, and the perils of deviance likewise consume the text of *Suddenly Last Summer,* first produced for the stage in 1958 and subsequently adapted into a film by director Joseph L. Mankiewicz in 1959.[5] Though much fodder has been made of *Suddenly Last Summer* by literary critics who have found the play's tone to be one of "barely repressed hysteria" (Paller 139), a historical overview of the play's reception would indicate the double-bind that Williams has received at the hands of his critical audience—he has been accused of being *too gay* by his contemporaries and *not gay enough* by more recent, post-Stonewall interpreters.[6]

If Williams' own authorial body fails to conform to expectations, the body of his text certainly betrays certain unruly tendencies as well. The play's phantom homosexual—the dead Sebastian Venable—may remain silent and never appear on stage in *Suddenly Last Summer,* not even through flashback, yet the disorder he causes cannot be fully contained within his own body either. Indeed, the entire play is haunted by Sebastian's absent presence. The diegesis of Williams' original text is confined to "Sebastian's garden" (Paller 37), a cramped, walled-in space to the side of Violet's house. Not surprisingly, literary critic John Clum sees the play's set as a symbol of repression—"a primal hothouse in a Victorian mansion" and as an "elaborate closet" (Clum 154)[7] that contains the action of the play. Yet Sebastian, even dead, has ways of coming out: as the true circumstances surrounding Sebastian's death emerge—he was torn limb from limb and partially cannibalized at the hands of an angry street mob of young Spanish boys whom he had sexually solicited—the only witness to Sebastian's death (his cousin Catharine) must work to prevent her own lobotomization at the hands of family members who wish to keep her quiet about the unseemly matter. Notions of dis-ease (and disease) abound here: indeed, Sebastian's condition is like a disease that spreads in ways that recall Artaud's formulations of theatre and plague as similar social and psychic constructions (15–32).[8] Williams exploits the contagious quality of theatricality in *Suddenly Last Summer*, as characters in the play and audience members alike face the threat of Sebastian's plague in its most Artaudian sense.[9]

To be sure, Sebastian's body is appropriately dis-oriented within the play. A stereotypical embodiment of some of the more common psychoanalytic theories of homosexuality at mid-century, Sebastian's relationship with his mother can be rendered topographically as being, quite frankly, *too close:* "I was actually the only one in his life that satisfied the demands he made of people," his mother Violet asserts to Doctor Cuckrowicz, Catharine's lobotomist-to-be (Williams 25). Violet continually speaks of her relationship with her son as one would speak about a romantic couple: "'Sebastian and Violet, Violet and Sebastian are staying at the Lido, they're at the Ritz in Madrid. Sebastian and Violet, Violet and Sebastian have taken a house in Biarritz for the season'" (25). Coupled with his father's *distance,* his mother's over-proximity makes for the perfect Oedpial recipe for Sebastian's queerness. The results of this orientation are only hinted at in the text of course, but Violet still suggests—no doubt unintentionally—its effects: she admits to Cukrowicz that, despite an outward posture of chastity, Sebastian had had "every kind of pursuer" (24), chasing him across Europe. Moreover, in the last year of his life, when Sebastian's queer tastes are explicitly revealed on the public beaches of Cabeza del Lobos, it seems appropriate that Sebastian's only reproductive capacity, his ability to produce poems, is lost.[10] If Violet's Freudian slips are not enough, Sebastian's failure to produce any offspring in his final days, even of the creative sort, effectively seals his fate as somehow oblique to the straight line of presumptively reproductive heterosexuality, in the terms of Ahmed's phenomenology.

And not only is the text haunted by Sebastian's queer presence, it is contaminated by that queerness as well. After Sebastian's death, Catharine Holly is the first body who becomes infected. Once Catharine witnesses Sebastian's death, she cannot stop talking about it. Violet first remarks about Catharine's condition by describing Catharine's behavior as sickness:

> She *babbles!* They couldn't shut her up in Cabeza de Lobo or at the clinic in Paris—she babbled, babbled!—smashing my son's reputation.—On the *Berengaria* bringing her back to the states she broke out of the stateroom and babbled; even at the airport when she was flown down here, she babbled a bit of her story before they could whisk her into an ambulance to St. Mary's. (Williams 27)[11]

After Catharine is infected by the queerness in Sebastian's body, her words have the power to infect others—even a "bit of her story" leaking out poses a threat in Violet's estimation. Should too many of Catharine's words "escape," the Venable family's reputation could be destroyed. The panic that Catharine's unruly, contagious body presents, the sheer anarchy it threatens, corresponds to Artaud's understanding of plague as producing disorder (both as chaos itself and as its own psychic or physical "dis-order" that would link appropriately to Ahmed's formulation of queer dis-orientation).[12] Because Catharine is now the source of contagion in the play, her unruly body comes to serve as a substitute for Sebastian's—and since Sebastian's body (already both literally and metaphorically perverted, now torn to pieces and cannibalized) can no longer be contained, Catharine's body simply must be.

Sara Ahmed's formulations on queer discomfort can further define Catharine's body as queer. In *Suddenly Last Summer,* Sebastian's body is dis-oriented—that is, sexually oriented towards bodies forbidden to it. Catharine's body too is dis-oriented: her love for Sebastian, her support of him in spite of his sexual appetite, has left her body similarly pulled in the wrong direction. (We could further argue that if queer is contagious, her very proximity to him might have infected her.) When Doctor Cuckrowicz indicates to Violet that her niece certainly appears "disturbed" in the garden (Williams 56), Catharine's disturbance signifies on multiple levels: she could be upset by her surroundings, by the threat of her continuing confinement at the asylum at Lion's View (itself an imposed spatial regulation of her unruly body)—or she could be more permanently emotionally or mentally "disturbed" somehow, off-kilter from the straight lines of her family tree through her relationship with Sebastian and her rumored dalliance with a married man. As her interrogation wears on, her brother George weighs in on the matter significantly: "She isn't crazy, Mama, she's no more crazy than I am. She's just, just—PERVERSE! Was ALWAYS!—perverse . . ." (47). Like Sebastian, Catherine too faces the designation of pervert. Her liason with a married man provides enough evidence of her capacity for sexual deviance, for living a life well out-of-line (64-5). With Sebastian dead, then, his queerness appropriately lives on in Catharine, Sebastian's closest companion.[13] Finally, both Catharine and Sebastian's bodies are simultaneously contaminated and uncontainable, and each character's uncontainability is always marked by the exceeding of a norm.[14] This exceeding, overflowing, even leaking adds to my phenomenological account of "orientation" within the text as these bodies simply refuse to remain within their expected confines or within the normative patterns of bodily arrangement prescribed to them.

Moreover, if queer movements resist the unwanted regulations of identity like disciplinary forces like categorization, de-realization, and de-legitimation, as Butler (among others) have argued (Butler 14), then Catharine's confession that comprises the climax of the play can be seen as her attempt to legitimate herself, or in Ahmed's terms, to "straighten" herself out. Crucially, as Catharine begins to tell the truth, she exposes not only Sebastian's deviant sexual orientation but also her own. She admits that Sebastian used her as a decoy for purposes of "procuring" (Williams 81) attractive "people"; the "people" (82) surrounding them at the café are eventually admitted to be "children" (83) and then specifically "boys," (88) as Catharine finally erupts (climaxes?) with what has been left unsaid. Moreover, along with this confession about Sebastian, Catharine confesses her attraction to Dr. Cukrowicz, her family-appointed physician: the sodium pentathol the doctor injects, a kind of injection-cum-penetration, leaves Catharine uninhibited, woozy, and assuredly heterosexual, causing her to swoon so the doctor can catch her and she can conveniently kiss him:

> Catharine: Let me! Let! Let! Let me! Let me, let me, oh, let me. . . .
>
> [*She crushes her mouth to his violently. He tries to disengage himself, She presses her lips to his fiercely, clutching his body against her. Her brother George enters.*]
>
> Please hold me! I've been so lonely. It's lonelier than death, if I've gone mad, it's lonelier than death! (Williams 71)

In a phenomenological worldview in which queerness registers as disturbance, disorientation, and dis-ease, dramatic resolution necessarily involves a return to the horizon line of heterosexuality like Catharine's. However, if Catherine's orientation seems to have corrected itself through her attempts at legitimation, one can surmise that the Doctor's sense of *dis*-orientation is only just beginning. Catharine's legitimacy may become assured through her heterosexual attraction for the unmarried doctor; yet after she absolves herself of any queerness by association, Catharine's revelation nonetheless leaves the doctor reeling, as he wonders, with a profound sense of the text's characteristically contagious dis(-)ease, what is false and what is true about her story at the end of the play.

If Catharine is the living protagonist of the play-text of *Suddenly Last Summer*, the focus nevertheless shifts away from her as the diegesis of the play is topographically expanded in the framework of the film.[15] One can consider the adaptation of text into film not only as a move across media, then, but as a geographic shift as well. No longer confined solely to Sebastian's closet/garden, new orientations between bodies and objects become possible under Mankiewicz's direction of Gore Vidal's screenplay. Therefore, it is unsurprising that on film we should see evidence of another queer infection taking place: here, Doctor's Cuckrowicz's body becomes the latest victim of the queer dis(-)ease, in ways the text itself can only hint at.

I suspect that some of Curcowicz's queerness on screen can be attributed to his being played by Montgomery Clift, a popular closeted 1950s non-straight actor who nonetheless ironically became a strong, heterosexual sex symbol in his day. From the beginning, then, Cukrowicz's body may already be queer. Regardless of the source of infection, though, Dr. Cukrowicz tries hard to hide all evidence of his dis(-)ease throughout the film—even as the film's screenplay almost conspires to work against him:

> Violet: You're very like him, Doctor.
>
> Doctor: In what way?
>
> Violet: You, a doctor, a surgeon, are dedicated to your art. Yes, an art—it *is* an art what you do, using people the way he did, grandly, creatively, almost like God.
>
> Doctor: I'm afraid my art is to help. Not to use but to be used.
>
> Violet: Well, it comes to the same end, doesn't it? I mean, in the end—oh, I don't know what I mean![16]

I need not push my reading of the screenplay too far to arrive at the double-entendres these lines suggest: it is repeatedly implied that Sebastian would have "liked" the good doctor and that the doctor "understood" what Sebastian was doing. Almost approaching the level of camp,[17] the passage above even suggests the doctor might like to *receive* rather than *give*, "in the end." Whether or not Violet [as played adroitly by Katherine Hepburn] knows what she means, the rest of us most certainly do. Moreover, if Catharine substitutes for Sebastian's body in the text, Cukrowicz's body certainly comes to substitute for Sebastian's on screen: though we do not see Sebastian's face in Catharine's flashbacks, we do receive glimpses of his body.[18] Sebastian is of middle height, tan, and thin, with dark hair—just as Clift / Dr. Cukrowicz is. It is no happy accident that, in the film's resolution, the screenplay departs from the lines of the text so that Violet goes mad after hearing Catharine's story. Violet actually mistakes Dr. Cukrowicz for Sebastian at the end of the *Suddenly* film, hallucinating that she is talking to her son on a boat in the Encantadas instead of talking to the doctor in her garden. This peculiar turn of events on film is orchestrated through Dr. Curcowicz's visual physical resemblance to Sebastian via Clift's portrayal. Does Violet understand more than we think at the end? Can she see the similarities between Sebastian's and the doctor's queer bodies? Like a contagion, queerness is transferred onto Cukrowicz's body in the film. And try as he might, he cannot shake off this infection—even when kissing the likes of Elizabeth Taylor.

In his scant treatment of *Suddenly Last Summer* in his landmark study, *The Celluloid Closet,* film historian Vito Russo evaluates the piece foremost as "Williams' tortured view of a failed homosexual artist and the people he victimizes in a classic horror story" (116). Certain conditions prevent the film's success for Russo: for instance, *Suddenly* is produced two years before homosexual subject matter is allowed on screen according to the rules of the Hays production code. Joseph L. Mankiewicz, the film's director, had to receive a special dispensation from the Breen office to go as far as he did on film—with an understanding that *Suddenly* would present a moral message to its viewers about the dangers of homosexuality. Perhaps too easily, however, Russo is able to stuff *Suddenly Last Summer* into the celluloid closet of its day, citing how contemporaneous films also treated homosexuality as "a dread disease" and that homosexuality could serve as "the kind of psychosexual freak show that the fifties almost demanded" (Russo, V. 116).

Importantly, Russo's use of words like "disease" and "freak" necessarily echo comments on the queer body as grotesque, excessive, and contagious that I have made earlier. Like much of the critical appraisal of the play itself, Russo's evaluation of the film finds *Suddenly Last Summer* a failure "that could not, in the end, explore its own subject" (Russo, V. 117). As influenced as I am by the work of Vito Russo, I must respectfully disagree with him here. Though roundly trashed by film reviewers, the *Suddenly Last Summer* film is brilliant in at least one respect: it is a glaring visual record of queerness as contagious dis-ease, uncontrollable dis-orientation. In this sense, I think the play does explore its own subject matter, and quite deftly.

The film's use of locations helps to accomplish such a feat. Rather than opening in Sebastian's walled closet-garden, the film's establishing shots are at the hospital where Cukrowicz works. From its beginning, then, the film sets up a series of spatial oppositions that regulate zones of habitability: those considered crazy or insane are free to wander the Drum, the hospital's asylum ward, but not to go out in the open. General mobility, and the freedom of movement between locations—and between scenes—are bodily orientations granted only to certain characters in the film. When Catharine and Cukrowicz finally do appear at Violet's mansion mid-way through the film, it's clear that they are both coded as being "out-of-place," one of the foremost geographical hallmarks of the queer condition.

Opening up the diegesis also helps the film to explore the text's treatment of *dis*-orientation. Violet's arrival on screen, for instance, constitutes an ironic play on orientation and re-orientation. She enters into frame by descending in an elaborately designed elevator, a contraption with no parallel in the text of the play. Violet explains her unusual entrance in this way: "Well it seems that the emperor of Byzantium, when he received people in audience, had a throne, which during the conversation would rise mysteriously in the air to the consternation of the visitors. But as we are living in a democracy, I reversed the procedure. I don't rise; I come down" (*Suddenly Last Summer*). In addition to dis-orienting viewers who might expect a more horizontal entrance on screen, Violet's "ride-on" is also a deliberate re-orientation of the Byzantine emperor's policies, a "reversal" of the procedure, as she says. Such a reversal suggests that other temporal and spatial re-orientations between bodies and objects, bodies and other bodies, are coming ahead. It might also help to suggest, as the text only begins to, that Violet may be another victim of the queer dis(-)ease, for the spatial re-orientation of the mise-en-scène she engineers overtly suggests the queer politics of sexual orientation that Ahmed writes about in her phenomenology. Certainly Violet is infected, as "the horrible death of Sebastian just about *killed* her!," Catharine's mother, Mrs. Holly, exclaims (Williams 44). The source of Violet's infection is not entirely clear, though. If Sebastian is wrongly oriented in his over-Oedipal relationship with his mother, Violet is just as guilty for keeping Sebastian *too close* to her own body. Violet might even have wound up infecting herself through her own alterations of proper spatial/familial relationships. Whatever the source of her dis(-)ease, the film begins to suggest her queer condition in ways beyond which the text of the play is capable.

The film's final scenes corroborate my suspicions that queerness is treated cinematographically as a non-standard orientation toward objects. Like the climax of the play, the climax of the film is the scene of Catharine's confession of truth. The increasing volume and tempo of the percussive music prepare the viewer for Catharine's scream, the emotional apex of the film. Appropriately, Catharine's scream dis-orients the viewer, as the camera work becomes slanted and renders her appropriately "off-kilter" with respect to the horizon line of the frame. We could certainly call this a queer scene, phenomenologically speaking. Ahmed writes that the normative can be considered an effect of repeating bodily actions over time, which produces what she calls the bodily horizon, a space for action that puts some objects in reach and others outside of reach. When normative re-orientation occurs, one's perspective becomes vertical once again with respect to the horizon line. As Ahmed writes, "we could describe heteronormativity as a straightening device which re-reads the 'slant' of queer desire" ("Orientations" 562).

Temporarily queered by Catharine's scream, the camera levels out when Catharine's flashback to Cabeza del Lobo ends and the cinematic apparatus turns its attention once again to Sebastian's garden in the "present day" of the film. As in the text of the play, Catharine's confession effects symbolic restoration on screen, for if Catharine's confession in the text legitimates her by revealing her as "straight" in the final outcome of events, the orientation of bodies at the end of the film visually corroborates her acceptance back into "normal" space. Alongside more "level" camerawork, Mrs. Holly now moves in to comfort Catharine for the first time, convinced that Catharine's deviance will no longer infect her with queerness. At this point in both the text and the film, Catharine is fully exposed, totally spent, her arduous trial finally over. Of course *her* queerness may no longer pose a threat, but the queer dis(-)ease has not yet been eradicated: in light of the reading I have offered, we can already suspect there are still a few other (closet?) cases littering *Suddenly Last Summer's* diegetic space.[19]

* * *

If discomfort is the hallmark of the queer condition, then being a graduate student may itself qualify as a queer existence through the dis(-)ease it so assiduously produces. Certainly, my current skin condition is not the sole source of my queer condition. Having submitted a draft of this essay to a professor in order to satisfy the requirements of a graduate seminar on gender, bodies, and affect, I found this in my inbox about halfway through my revisions of the piece for its publication:

> Bradley,
>
> I congratulate you on trying something different. I'm not sure it's fully working at the moment, but most-risk taking requires several attempts in order to achieve success. My overall sense of the relation between your self-reflective passages and the analysis of *Suddenly Last Summer* is that they don't always work in complementary ways. Now I know that you like the idea of disjunction and dis-ease for your reader, but you do want some motivated relationship between the two parts. Queering the text is one thing, but confusing it is another.
>
> Also, when you are actually in the *SLS* sections, you no longer work in a "queer" way, meaning it moves into a pretty conventional literary analysis that interrogates queer sexuality rather than an actual *queer* analysis of the literature. That may be fine if you want to work as such, but it did strike me that your experimentation was limited.
>
> I did find myself a bit confused about what it is you wanted me to understand at the end of your piece. I do get the discomfort point, but I still need a clearer statement of intent as it relates to *SLS*.
>
> Grade: A-

* * *

In the Acknowledgments to her 2004 collection, *Undoing Gender*, Judith Butler notes the particular role that Gayle Salamon, one of her graduate students, had on encouraging her to rethink her position on materiality and embodiment. Gayle Salamon's work uses some of Butler's earlier writing, especially *Bodies that Matter*, in order to address what psychoanalysis can bring to bear on modern discussions of embodiment and gender. Provocatively, Salamon maintains that "both body and psyche are characterized by their ability rather than their ability to contain" (108), and credits Butler in kind with helping her to see how the material body is not overlaid with a social layer, but rather that both the material body and the social realm emerge simultaneously in a phenomenological sense (114). Salmon's theories provide a necessary link, then, between Ahmed's theory of queerness as phenomenological embodiment and certain psychoanalytic concepts I treat below that influence my response to the queerness of *Suddenly Last Summer.*

Though Salamon is primarily interested in what psychoanalysis can say about transgender life within contemporary discussions of embodiment and gender (95), she also devotes a lot of attention to conceptions of a bodily ego in ways that may be useful to broader theoretical projects that incorporate psychoanalytic theory. Foremost, she insists on the relevance of a psychoanalytic approach to embodiment: "Since psychoanalysis deals with the psychic construction of the self and the way in which that self inhabits a body, it can complicate the assumption that the material body is unproblematically available to us as a perfectly faithful reflection of the psychic self" (95–96). As she explores the Kleinian concepts of the bodily ego and the use to which it has been put by writers who grapple with questions of gender, body, and identity, she would suggest, alongside Ahmed's claim that "one is not born, but rather becomes straight,"[20] "one is not born a body, but becomes one" as well (Salamon 105). Salamon builds this argument by inserting herself into the discursive history of projection as a psychoanalytic term,[21] ultimately arguing that both the "body" and the "ego" must be thought of as effects of projection.

My brief deviation into psychoanalysis (and the pedagogical role graduate students might sometimes play for their own professors) is not mere whimsy on my part; projection becomes particularly useful for theorizing how queerness circulates as a kind of contagious affect in *Suddenly Last Summer*, particularly in light of Kleinian work on the role of projection in identification—in Klein's terms, projective identification.[22] Though Klein is initially concerned with how patients project content to manage their own identities, Klein's student and analysand Wilfred Bion has perhaps worked the most productively of anyone with Klein's account of projective identification by reorienting it (Ahmed might even say queering it) to target the therapist.[23] Bion perceives how the therapist can become a "container" (Mitchell and Black 104), for mental content originating in the experiences of the patient, especially in moments he describes when the therapist experiences "a temporary loss of insight . . . without recourse to recondite explanation" (Bion, *Experiences* 149). When the therapist cannot otherwise make an interpretation, Bion insists he can use what the patient projects onto him as a guide, even using his own cognitive disorientation as a productive symptom of the counter-transference.

The momentary dis-orientation that Bion describes seems particularly fruitful to my consideration of queerness in *Suddenly Last Summer*, especially since, in their history of psychoanalytic thought, Mitchell and Black explicitly tie projective identification to phenomena of contagious affect (105). Processes of projective identification, then, can begin to explain exactly *how* queerness circulates like an affective contagion of dis(-)ease and discomfort in the text and the film. In both versions of *Suddenly Last Summer*, the impacts of projective identification are made visible: Dr. Cuckrowicz's relation to Catharine bears traces of projective exchanges. He insists to her, "Give me all your resistance. See. I'm holding my hand out. I want you to put yours in mine and give me all your resistance. Pass all your resistance out of your hand to mine" (Mitchell and Black 105). Such remarks highlight the possibilities for transference that organize the analytic experience.

Despite the suggestive potential of such relations, however, the most important projective exchanges in *Suddenly Last Summer* are those between Sebastian and the characters he "infects." Notably, Catharine becomes an obvious container for Sebastian's own queer experiences as a result of his projective impulses upon her—notice how Sebastian's emotional states, even some aspects of his self, are taken in and sometimes even intensified by Catharine: "He liked me and so I loved him" (Williams 40), "he was affectionate with me, so sweet and attentive to me, that some people took us for a honeymoon couple . . . he bought me so many new clothes that. . . . I turned into a peacock! Of course, so was *he* too . . ." (74). Catharine, Violet, even Dr. Cuckrowicz take in Sebastian's queerness until their very *positions* within the work become queer.[24] Provocatively, then, it would appear that theorizing projective identification requires a complementary theory of object relations.[25] Kleinian object-relations theory suffices for intra-psychic processes, while Ahmed's queer phenomenology could account for the social arrangement of bodies in space. Take both theories together and a surprising insight occurs to me: ironically, queerness may boil down to *object* choices after all.

My interest in projective identification is not solely confined to the text itself, though. If we take Kleinian-Bionic theories of projective identification seriously, the relationship between reader and text would allow for transference and counter-transference alike. (It is likely not accidental that Klein first explained her theory of projective identification by undertaking the reading of a novel herself [Klein, "On Identification" 145–63].) I could therefore use contemporary Kleinian-Bionic formation of projective identification not only to understand how queerness works as contagious affect in the text and the film versions of *Suddenly Last Summer*—I could also apply the concept to see how my own response to the works continue to spread queerness. Here then, may be an answer to the question my professor posed in her feedback to me: my reading moves from a reading of queerness in *Suddenly Last Summer* to a "queer" reading of the text through my own internalization of the text's contagious, dis-orienting queerness. From a contemporary Kleinian-Bionic perspective, the analyst's own experience of counter-transference can become a vehicle for grasping segments of a patient's life, particularly when she or he utilizes the communicative dimensions of projective identification to generate hypotheses about the organization of the patient's experience (Mitchell and Black 110). What if my response to the versions of *Suddenly Last Summer* worked in a similar way? How have I internalized the queerness of the texts? How has my own body been reoriented (and queered) as a result of my reading?[26]

* * *

"You *are* an odd case."

"Oh, really? How's that?"

A week after the end of the semester, I was no better. The itching continued, got worse even, as my body started to develop lines and patches of violet and red. The lotions weren't working, so I was back to the health center. This time I got a doctor, instead of the nurse.

"Well, if it was hives, or anxiety, or even eczema, it wouldn't look like this. Maybe you've been infected with something. . . ."

"*Infected*?"

"Scabies would be my guess."

"How do you know if I have it?"

"Well, I'll give you the scabies treatment, and if you get better, that means you probably had it. Is there anyone you could have caught it from? Or given it to? You'll have to wash all your clothes, your bedding, anything you've had prolonged contact with. That could be why you're not any better—you could be continually re-contaminating yourself."

"Well, there's my boyfriend. I guess my boyfriend should come in to get checked out too, in that case. If it *is* scabies, we could re-infect each other, right?"

"Oh—um—yes, I guess so. Scabies can pass between roommates sometimes."

"Ok, I'll tell him he needs to come in too. Can he request to see you specifically?"

"Oh. Um, you don't have to do that. I'll—. . . I'll just write you two prescriptions. One for you and one for your roommate. If it's not that, you should probably come in and get screened for other kinds of infections, too. You could have *anything*, really. . . ."

* * *

For multiple reasons, I write this chapter full of discomfort. My body is itching, dry, swollen, and sleep-deprived and (also? consequently?) queer. I write from the uneasy position of being a queer graduate student, in a profession that is often ill-at-ease with my very presence. My body—and my body of work—are often thought to be unruly. The discomfort that my queerness creates, both in my own body and in the bodies of those around me, urges me to keep adjusting myself, to keep moving, to find new ways of orienting myself and to seek relief for what is sore and raw, even if that relief is momentary.

To be sure, *Suddenly Last Summer* does not mark the beginning of the discourse of queer dis(-)ease, nor does it mark the end of it. The queer dis(-)ease persists; I manifest its symptoms and feel its effects. I offer the parts of this chapter to you, pieced together, in the spirit of *dis*-orientation. What I have offered is not only a *queer* reading of the play's adaption, but also a psychoanalytic reading of queerness in both the text and the film, with queerness defined as a phenomenological experience of embodied (dis-)orientation. My own narratives serve as a record of the ways in which I have either internalized the queerness of the play and the film through processes of projective identification (rather than sheer mental masturbation, is my own self-cannibalism nothing more than a queer intellectual attempt at auto-fellatio?), or else projected my own queerness onto and into the arrangement of objects in both texts (my willful determination to read Montgomery Clift as queer in the movie, for instance). Most likely, this chapter is a narrative of both processes, my own queer kind of reader-(call-and)response.

This montage is a deliberate arrangement, then, about my *relation,* or my orientation, if you will, to this particular archive, as well as about my *location* within the larger academy. Perhaps due to the queer positions I find myself in, I must admit my vision is fragmented. I can only write and talk, dodge and move, confessing, at times perhaps extruding what is 'inside' me out into the open to provoke the discomfort of those around me. Of course I cannot predict the possibilities of my future academic career, nor can I foresee the lives of hope and possibility that I pray future queer generations will experience. Instead, I must content myself at the moment with scratching the surface of my own body, and occasionally glimpsing the potential my contortions can offer to queer bodies that are, perhaps, somehow like mine.

NOTES

1. Butler also explores her own discomfort with "queer" in "Changing the Subject: Judith Butler's Politics of Radical Resignification," an interview with Gary A. Olson and Lynn Worsham, *JAC: A Journal of Composition Theory* 20:4 (2000): 731-6, and in *Excitable Speech: A Politics of the Performative.* New York: Routledge, 1997, especially 103–26.

2. On the use of personal narrative in academic writing, see Julia Emberley, "Body Interrupted: Textual Montage, Traumatized Bodies, and the De-disciplining of Knowledge"; C. Ellis & A. P. Bochner, "Autoethnography, Personal Narrative, Reflexivity: Researcher as Subject"; Linda Brodkey, *Writing Permitted in Designated Areas Only*; and Janet L. Miller, "Autobiography as a Queer Curricular Practice."

3. My use of disease acknowledges an understanding of disease in much of the cultural production of the Victorian period, even as I call for a postmodern analysis of the gendered and sexualized dimensions of such constructions of embodiment in the present in specifically queer terms. See for instance Pamela K. Gilbert, *Disease,*

Desire, and the Body in Victorian Women's Popular Novels. Cambridge: Cambridge UP, 1997, where Gilbert suggests that capitalist expansion during Victorian urbanization was culturally represented as a kind of "dangerous intercourse" (12) that could infect or damage participants through uneven or inappropriate exchanges specifically defined through sexual metaphors. Gilbert explores how understandings contagion in the Victorian period were inflected through gender (through the feminization of the diseased body), sexuality (through an interest in the sexually-transmitted infection), and empire. Midcentury and twenty-first century American cultures offer a discrete discursive organization of contagion and the body that are nonetheless historically linked to such cultural representations.

4. In her more recent work on queer phenomenology, "Orientations: Towards a Queer Phenomenology," and, in expanded form, in *Queer Phenomenology*. Durham: Duke UP, 2006, Ahmed becomes even more consumed with the materiality of the body. Ahmed turns to phenomenology because it is the branch of philosophy that makes notions of *orientation* most central to its work, through a fundamental argument that consciousness is always directed toward objects and hence is always worldly, situated, and, in turn, *embodied* (see "Orientations" 544). Enlarging upon her formulation of queer as a kind of dis-orientation, Ahmed suggests more recently that *all* sexual "orientation" is foremost a matter of residence, of how we inhabit spaces. With heterosexuality topologized as "straightness" in her phenomenological account of sexuality, Ahmed is able to show how "one is not born, but rather *becomes* straight" (544). She further explains, "To become straight means not only that we have to turn toward the objects given to us by heterosexual culture but also that we must turn away from objects that take us off this line" (554).

5. Quotations from the text are from Tennessee Williams, *Suddenly Last* Summer. New York: Signet, 1976; quotations from the screenplay of the film are taken directly from *Suddenly Last Summer*. Dir. Joseph L. Mankiewicz. Columbia Pictures, 1959.

6. Compare Paller with Christopher Conlon's "'Fox-Teeth in Your Heart': Sexual Self-Portraiture in the Poetry of Tennessee Williams." In Conlon's model of critical reception, one assumes that Williams wrote *Suddenly Last Summer* as a kind of morality play about the problem of homosexuality and that Williams uses the stage to work through issues regarding his own sexuality. Such interpretations depend heavily on Williams' own biography and are limited in their applicability outside of searching for correspondences between Williams' own life and the lives of his characters. Paller shows how readings like Conlon's have merely tended to recall comments from earlier eras that accused the play of failing due to its own excesses (Paller 146).

7. In *Epistemology of the Closet*, Eve Sedgwick has convincingly argued that the notion of the closet proves fundamental to understandings of gay identity (the construction of which actually requires the existence of a closet); and, moreover, that the closet has had a broad impact on Western culture and history at large (68).

8. Using medieval stories of the bubonic plague as a starting point, Artaud argues that the crisis which plagues provoke cannot be fully accounted for by a virus: "The plague microbe as a smaller—infinitely smaller—material element which appears at some moment in the development of the virus, but which in no way accounts for the plague" (21). Artaud sees the social and psychic dimensions of disease in his

understanding of plague, which allows him to equate plague with the loss of control and the threat of anarchy. If threats of plague do not necessarily depend on viral microbes for their transmission, it becomes apparent how the threat Sebastian poses to the social order in *Suddenly Last Summer* becomes contagious. Furthermore, plays produce their own kind of contagion for Artaud, threats of panic or delirium that can spread through the audience and attack customs rather than bodies.

9. It is this possibility for infection that plays featuring the homosexuality unexpectedly exploit in Williams' era: In *Acting Gay: Male Homosexuality in Modern Drama*, Clum pays particular attention to the figure of homosexual in American drama during the 1950s and 1960s. During that period, a particular figure of the male homosexual begins to emerge on stage such that homosexual characters both defy and reconfigure characteristics of the traditional "American dream." In Clum's words, "mainstream realist drama exploited the melodramatic potential of homosexuality while enforcing norms of heterosexuality and conventional notions of masculinity by raising the possibility of homosexuality but never showing a homosexual character" (141). This convention of raising the constant threat of homosexuality without ever visibly exposing it works to create "closet drama" (149), a genre that can hint at the possibility of the homosexual taboo and deny such a possibility at the same time. It is easy to see how such a staging of homosexuality might then devolve into "barely repressed hysteria," as Paller mentions (see note 8, above)—I would argue that the discursive environment of closet drama succeeded precisely to the extent that it produced such results.

10. Violet refers to Sebastian's preparation to write his yearly *Poem of Summer* as "the length of a pregnancy" (Williams 15). During his last summer, Sebastian was unable to start his poem, thus failing to give birth to his life's work.

11. Catharine's disordered talking is ironically similar to cases of melancholia in the psychoanalytic literature where patients over-speak but say nothing. I thank Jes Battis for pointing out that such a behavior is a queer form of repression itself, further testifying to the discursive organization of queerness in the play-text as a fundamentally affective form of contagion.

12. A modern application of Artaud can be found in Jackie Orr, *Panic Diaries: A Genealogy of Panic Disorder*. Orr relies heavily on metaphors of performance and contagion in her study of panic disorder as she applies Artaud's essay on "The Theatre and the Plague" into a broader cultural analysis in which panic becomes "floating attacks of terror that occur without any apparent cause" (11), affecting people like a contagious form of theatrical delirium akin to Artaud's understanding of the theater of cruelty. These metaphors become useful as Orr bridges Artaud's sense of theatricality to Freudian understandings of hysteria as performance, and as she extends Artaud's interest in theater-as-plague to increasingly somatic, cybernetic, and pharmacological accounts of mental disorder in contemporary psychiatry. Orr's extension of Artaud into the contemporary mental health industry directly influences my own analysis of contemporary psychiatric diagnoses of queer conditions.

13. In fact, Catherine and Sebastian's forms of deviance are remarkably similar, each disciplined by regulatory arenas like psychiatry (Catharine's lobotomy would lessen the effects of her ostensible schizophrenia; Sebastian's homosexuality would be classified as a mental illness by the APA until 1973); the law (if Sebastian is a pervert, Catherine is a "vandal" [26] who will destroy the family's image); and the

system of criminal justice (enacting homosexual sex and "procuring" [81] for it would each be criminal offenses).

14. In *The Femail Grotesque: Risk, Excess, and Modernity*, Mary Russo incorporates such an understanding of containability into her characterization of the grotesque, namely as that which is significantly "open, protruding, irregular, secreting, multiple, and changing" (7). For the purposes of this project, the grotesque body as a psychiatric patient has its own long discursive history: Mary Russo notes Freud's dependence on the grotesque through his use of "creature feature" case studies and underscores that subjectivity as it is understood in the West requires an image of the grotesque body (9); psychoanalytic theorist Gayle Salamon as much as confirms Russo's claim when she writes about the material body, "body can and does exceed its own skin. Both body and psyche are characterized by their lability, rather than their ability to contain" (108). Hence, it is more than fitting that in *Suddenly Last Summer* Catharine Venable's body should threaten to erupt at any moment!

15. The 1959 adaptation of *Suddenly Last Summer* to the screen is of interest for this analysis of queer dis(-)ease for several reasons. The particular conditions of the film's production suggest some of my fascination with the film: *Suddenly Last Summer* is a purportedly a "problem play" about homosexuality, written by a gay playwright, adapted for the screen by gay writer Gore Vidal, and starring a closeted gay leading man, in which 1) the word "homosexuality" may not be uttered due to the production code, 2) the gay central character is never seen on screen, and 3) gay actor Montgomery Clift must accordingly play it "straight" by serving as a love interest to Elizabeth Taylor's Catharine Venable. The film's production conditions, coupled with source material of Williams' play, combine to make sexuality paradoxically both completely repressed and completely over-expressed on screen.

16. Other lines from the film's screenplay do just as good a job of allowing the queer meanings I suggest. Compare:

> Violet: [*to the doctor*] Such extraordinary eyes—just like his. You must—I almost said you must meet my son Sebastian. (*Suddenly Last Summer*)
>
> * * *
>
> Doctor: Why [did Sebastian do it]? Because he thought you were lonely? Did he think he could shock you out of your depression?
> Catharine: *You* know why he was doing it. I told you I was procuring for him. (*Suddenly Last Summer*)

17. Camp aesthetics have long had a discursive relationship with "queer." In "Introduction: Queering the Camp," Fabio Cleto asserts camp's inability to be pinned down and overviews its varying treatments as a sensibility, a style, an aesthetic or cultural economy, and finally as a queer discourse. For an application of camp aesthetics to the work of Tennessee Williams, see James Francis, "Camping Out: Sexuality as Aesthetic Value in Tennessee Williams's *And Tell Sad Stories of the Deaths of Queens . . .*"

18. Laura Mulvey's influential "Visual Pleasure and Narrative Cinema" first established the now-familiar argument in feminist film that men serve as the protagonists in classic Hollywood cinema and that it is the job of female characters

to "stand still and look pretty," in what she perceives as a narrative/spectacle split that corresponds to the male/female binary. As an artifact situated squarely within the studio system of Classical Hollywood Cinema, the film version of *Suddenly Last Summer* conforms such an analysis. Early shots in the film introduce the viewer to Dr. Cukrowicz apart from the Venable family. His expertise in medicine and the financial troubles his hospital faces are confirmed before viewers ever visit Violet's garden in the film. His character's financial motivation for performing the lobotomy—Violet volunteers to donate a hefty sum to support his future work—is thoroughly established before Catharine is ever introduced. For these reasons, then, it may be more accurate to argue, despite what one might suppose, that it is Cukrowicz rather than Catharine who is the protagonist of the film.

19. Violent Venable is the most likely candidate here, and not merely because she is played in the film by Katherine Hepburn. Violet's own relationship with her son borders on the incestuous, at least psychoanalytically speaking. Her psychosexual deviance may intensify what ever dis-ease circulates within the play. On Hepburn's status as a queer cultural symbol, see Alexander Doty, *Making Things Perfectly Queer*. Minneapolis: University of Minnesota Press, 1993, especially 17–38.

20. See note 6, above.

21. Freud saw ego identification as a part of normal development that followed early processes of introjection; following Freud, Melanie Klein revised available understandings of identification to suggest the major importance of certain *projective* mechanisms which are complimentary to the introjective ones Freud described. For more information see Klein, "On Identification," as well as Stephen A. Mitchell and Margaret J. Black, *Freud and Beyond: A History of Modern Psychoanalytic,* 101.

22. Klein eventually arrived at the concept of projective identification to describe the processes by which an ego projects not only discrete impulses but also entire parts of the self into others, where the ego then struggles to keep some connection to and control over that content. See Klein, "On Identification."

23. Bion became interested in projection through his concern in the impact of projective identification not only in the ego that projects content, but also the person onto whom the content is projected. Based on his own experiences with schizophrenic patients, Bion found he would have intense affective reactions to his patients that could not be fully understood by him as reactions of empathy. Much more mystical than other Kleinians, Bion would abjure a strictly scientistic understanding of analysis. In *Attention and Interpretation,* Bion suggests that, when faced with a number of equally compelling interpretations, the analyst "is forced to choose what interpretation to give." Earlier, in *Experiences in Groups,* Bion writes, "in group treatment, many interpretations, and amongst them the most important, have to be made on the strength of the analyst's own emotional reactions. It is my belief that these reactions are dependent on the fact that the analyst in the group is at the receiving end of what Melanie Klein has called projective identification, and that this mechanism plays a very important role in groups. Now the experience of counter-transference appears to me to have quite a distinct quality that should enable the analyst to differentiate the occasion when he is the object of a projective identification from the occasion when he is not" (149).

24. This should not appear so surprising, particularly when one considers that Klein initially considered projective identification from three specific angles: "1) the

relation of the split-off and projected parts of his personality to those he left behind; 2) the motives underlying the choice of objects into whom he projects himself; and 3) how far in these processes the projected part of his self becomes submerged in the objects or gains control over it" (Klein, "On Identification" 168). Notice Klein's particular attention to 'objects,' spatial distance, and levels of topography—this is an attention that Ahmed would certainly appreciate too.

25. Klein admits as much when she writes that "[i]dentification by projection implies a combination of splitting off parts of the self and projecting them on to (or rather into) another person. These processes have many ramifications and fundamentally influence object relations" ("On Identification" 143), especially those process that form part of the paranoid-schizoid position. For more information, see Klein's essay "Notes on Some Schizoid Mechanisms."

26. My treatment of *Suddenly Last Summer* thus far has almost completely avoided the subject of cannibalism, for instance. Psychoanalytically speaking, one could interpret my disavowal of the text's cannibalism as symptomatic, if not utterly ironic, especially since I seem to be cannibalizing my own earlier readings of the play (as well as my own personal experiences) to arrive at a final draft of this essay. Using Kleinian-Bionic theories of projective identification, one could suggest that I have previously ignored the cannibalism of the text precisely *because* I have introjected it. The text's cannibalism may be oblivious to me because it no longer resides in the text; it resides in me instead. Moreover, perhaps my inattention to cannibalism in my reading of *Suddenly Last Summer* above is actually about my own discomfort with the queerest and most abject parts of myself. Perhaps my lack of attention to the text's cannibalism enacts some fantasy of mine that there would be some topic *too* queer or too grotesque even for me to discuss, some queerness that is off-limits even to *my* queer body. Or perhaps, as my professor suggests, I'm not as queer as I want to be after all.

BIBLIOGRAPHY

Ahmed, Sara. *The Cultural Politics of Emotion*. New York: Routledge, 2004.

———. "Orientations: Towards a Queer Phenomenology." *GLQ* 12.4 (2006): 543–74.

Artaud, Antonin. *The Theatre and Its Double*. New York: Grove, 1958.

Berlant, Lauren, with Elizabeth Freeman. "Queer Nationality." *The Queen of America Goes to Washington City: Essays of Sex and Citizenship*. Durham: Duke UP, 2002. 145–74.

Bion, W. B. *Experiences in Groups*. New York: Basic Books, 1959.

———. *Attention and Interpretation: A Scientific Approach to Insight in Psycho-Analysis and Groups*. New York: Basic Books, 1970.

Brodkey, Linda. *Writing Permitted in Designated Areas Only*. Minneapolis: University of Minnesota Press, 1996.

Butler, Judith. "Critically Queer." *Playing with Fire: Queer Politics, Queer Theories*. Ed. Shane Phelan. New York: Routledge, 1997. 11–31.

———. *Undoing Gender*. New York: Routledge, 2004.

Cleto, Fabio. "Introduction: Queering the Camp." *Camp: Queer Aesthetics and the Performing Subject*. Ann Arbor: University of Michigan Press, 1999. 1–44.

Clum, John. *Acting Gay: Male Homosexuality in Modern Drama.* New York: Columbia UP, 1992.

Conlon, Christopher. "'Fox-Teeth in Your Heart': Sexual Self-Portraiture in the Poetry of Tennessee Williams." *The Tennessee Williams Annual Review* 4 (2001): 59–70.

Ellis, C. and A. P. Bochner. "Autoethnography, Personal Narrative, Reflexivity: Researcher as Subject." *Handbook of Qualitative Research.* 2nd ed. Ed. N. K. Denzin and Y. S. Lincoln. Thousand Oaks: Sage, 2000. 733–68.

Emberley, Julia. "Body Interrupted: Textual Montage, Traumatized Bodies, and the Dedisciplining of Knowledge." *Resources for Feminist Research* 29.3 & 4 (2002): 69–84.

Foucault, Michel. *The History of Sexuality, Volume 1: An Introduction.* New York: Vintage, 1977.

Francis, James. "Camping Out: Sexuality as Aesthetic Value in Tennessee Williams's *And Tell Sad Stories of the Deaths of Queens. . .*" *The Tennessee Williams Annual Review 10*: 131–42.

Klein, Melanie. "Notes on Some Schizoid Mechanisms." *Envy and Gratitude and Other Works, 1946–1963: The Writings of Melanie Klein.* Vol. 3. New York: Delacorte, 1975. 1–24.

——. "On Identification." *Envy and Gratitude and Other Works, 1946–1963: The Writings of Melanie Klein.* Vol. 3. New York: Delacorte, 1975. 141–75.

Kupers, Terry. "The Politics of Psychiatry: Gender and Sexual Preference in DSM-IV." *Questions of Gender: Perspectives and Paradoxes.* Ed. Dina L. Anselmi and Anne L. Law. Boston: McGraw Hill, 1998. 759–66.

Miller, Janet L. "Autobiography as a Queer Curricular Practice." *Queer Theory in Education.* Ed. William B. Pinar. Mahwah: Erlbaum, 1998. 365–73.

Mitchell, Stephen A. and Margaret J. Black. *Freud and Beyond: A History of Modern Psychoanalytic Thought.* New York: Basic Books, 1995.

Mulvey, Laura. "Visual Pleasure and Narrative Cinema." *Screen 16* (1975): 6–18.

Orr, Jackie. *Panic Diaries: A Genealogy of Panic Disorder.* Durham: Duke UP, 2005.

Paller, Michael. *Gentleman Callers: Tennessee Williams, Homosexuality, and Mid-Twentieth-Century American Drama.* New York: Palgrave, 2005.

Russo, Mary. *The Female Grotesque: Risk, Excess, and Modernity.* New York: Routledge, 1994.

Russo, Vito. *The Celluloid Closet: Homosexuality in the Movies.* New York: Harper and Row, 1985.

Salamon, Gayle. "The Bodily Ego and the Contested Domain of the Material." *differences* 15.3 (2004): 95–122.

Sedgwick, Eve Kosofsky. *The Epistemology of the Closet.* Berkeley: University of California Press, 1990.

——. *Tendencies.* Durham: Duke UP, 1993.

Suddenly Last Summer. Dir. Joseph L. Mankiewicz. Columbia Pictures, 1959.

Williams, Tennessee. *Suddenly Last Summer.* New York: Signet, 1976.

Index

About the Contributors

Billy Clem is a PhD candidate in English and women's studies at Northern Illinois University and works as associate professor of English at Waubonsee Community College where he teaches writing, multiculturalism, women's studies, and disability studies. His critical and creative work have appeared in *MELUS*, *Lodestar Quarterly*, *Moon City Review*, and *Elder Mountain*.

Brianne Colon is currently completing her thesis, entitled "Privy Information: Toilets and Theatrical Spectatorship from the Elizabethan to the Eighteenth-Century Stage," which focuses on the social ramifications of spectatorial abjection and earned her a 2009 SSHRC Graduate Scholarship. Her main research areas include early modern drama, gender and sexuality, theatre architecture, and Canadian print culture.

Marty Fink is a doctoral candidate in the English department of the Graduate Center of the City University of New York. Her current work traces queer histories of resistance to HIV/AIDS. Fink currently resides in Montreal where she is involved with AIDS Community Care Montreal and with the Prisoner Correspondence Project: www.prisonercorrespondenceproject.com

Loren Krywanczyk teaches English at a public middle school in Brooklyn. He also teaches middle school students at Bank Street School of Education and graduate students at Pace University.

Bradley Lane researches contemporary feminist and queer visual cultures, as well as the cultural politics of American sexuality. He is presently earning his PhD in gender studies from Indiana University, with a dissertation project that concerns the visual representation of sexual perversion, particularly through the figure of the sexual predator. Previously, Bradley has served as a lecturer in women's and gender studies at Vanderbilt University and a contributor to *LGBT America Today*. He is presently Core Faculty in Humanities for Seattle Community Colleges.

Em McAvan is an honourary research postdoctoral associate at Murdoch University in Perth, Australia and has published on religion, literature, and gender studies.

Jennifer Mitchell is a doctoral candidate in English literature at the CUNY Graduate Center. She is currently writing her dissertation about the intersections of sexology and literature, and working on several other projects involving masochism, psychoanalysis, 19th and early 20th century British literature, theories of gender and sexuality, and any combination of the above. She teaches Victorian literature and children's literature at Hunter College.

Marcos Moldes is a graduate student in the School of Communication at Simon Fraser University, where he works on questions of identity and the regulation of identity.

C. Riley Snorton is a PhD candidate at the Annenberg School for Communication at The University of Pennsylvania. He is currently completing his dissertation, "Trapped in the [Epistemological] Closet: Black Sexuality and the Popular Imagination," which examines representations of the "down low," a term that refers to black men who have sex with men and women and do not identify as gay or bisexual, in news and popular culture.

Nicholas Wright is a graduate student in the Department of English at SUNY-New Paltz.